D0333421

A Time to Reflect

A TIME TO REFLECT

365 Classic Meditations
to help you through the year

Compiled by Henry Morgan

A LION BOOK

Compilation copyright © 1998 Henry Morgan
This edition copyright © 1998 Lion Publishing

Published by
Lion Publishing plc
Sandy Lane West, Oxford, England
www.lion-publishing.co.uk
ISBN 0 7459 4033 1

First edition 1998
10 9 8 7 6 5 4 3 2 1 0

All rights reserved

A catalogue record for this book is available
from the British Library

Typeset in 11.75/14.5 Goudy OldStyle
Printed and bound in Great Britain by
Biddles Ltd, Guildford & King's Lynn

CONTENTS

INTRODUCTION

God begins everything. When we seek God it is not we ourselves who initiate this quest. Rather, it is God who initiates it in us. So whatever impulse it was that led you to pick up this book, open it and begin to read; it was God who implanted that impulse in you. You are seeking something, and it is God who has called you to seek. Whether you will find what you are seeking in the pages of this book, or elsewhere, that I don't know! But that your seeking was initiated by God, of that I have no doubt.

As Maria Boulding wrote: 'God creates in human hearts a huge desire and a sense of need, because he wants to fill them with the gift of himself. It is because his self-sharing love is there first, forestalling any response or prayer from our side, that such hope can be in us. We cannot hope until we know, however obscurely, that there is something to hope for; if we have had no glimpse of a vision, we cannot conduct our lives with vision. And yet we do: there is hope in us, and longing, because grace was there first. God's longing for us is the spring of ours for him.' (*The Coming of God*, SPCK, 1994)

One of the strange ironies of the times in which we live, is that there seems to be a great outpouring of God's longing for us, and a consequent great searching for God on our part; while the Christian churches seem almost completely preoccupied with other agenda of their own! Everybody is the loser here. The churches need this Spirit-led enthusiasm for exploration, to breathe new life into them: and those who are searching need to be in touch with the traditional wisdom, of which the churches are the guardians. But the meeting rarely seems to take place. This little book is a very modest attempt to bring the two sides together: a bridge perhaps where they can meet.

Over the course of one year, it contains readings from across the Christian tradition, with each month focusing on a different aspect. Not all parts of the tradition can be covered in such a small span; and the tradition has been understood fairly widely to embrace readings that might otherwise have been omitted; while some readings could easily have found themselves in any of several homes. The lines drawn here are not hard and fast. The aim has been to offer a reasonable sample of the riches and range of the tradition on the one hand, and the breadth that must accompany authentic exploring, on the other. It is a constant source of delight to watch while God calls someone, and then to see them set out on a journey which takes in places both familiar and strange. God is nothing if not full of surprises!

A few tips for the journey. First, journeying with God towards God requires a balance of activity and passivity. You have to be prepared to knock on a few doors, to try some new things. But you also have to be prepared sometimes just to wait, to be patient. Most of the things that you will need for your journey will come and find you; you don't have to find them. You just have to recognize them when they come by. More often than not they will be other than what you expected. Remember the Gospel stories of the Risen Lord coming to his followers: usually they did not recognize him at first, and when recognition had taken place, the person met was both strange and strangely familiar. So it may well be for you.

This is a book of meditations from the Christian tradition, but it contains a small number of pieces by people who may be surprised to see themselves thought of in that way. I have included them partly because of the quality of what they had written, whatever their tradition; and partly to make the point that God may speak to any of us through people seemingly from outside our tradition. Angels (God's messengers) don't wear 'party colours'!

Second, there are no such things as mistakes on this journey, just learning opportunities. You won't always get it right, even supposing that you think you know what 'right' is. But we are dealing with a loving and forgiving God, and the best way of learning is through making 'mistakes'. So take the journey seriously, but not too seriously.

Third, you will be helped enormously, by having someone with whom you can share your experience of the spiritual journey. Traditionally such a person is called a spiritual director, or a spiritual friend. The name sounds a little heavy, but they are someone you can meet with from time to time to reflect on where God seems to be taking you. It is easy to misread the signs on the way, and quite possible to deceive yourself, so having someone who is already an experienced spiritual traveller, just to check things out with, is invaluable. And the whole thing feels less lonely.

Which takes me to my fourth point. It is very easy, but a grave mistake, to let your journey become a solitary and individualist affair. It is important for your journey to have a corporate element to it, for it to be something which, in some way, you share with others. Traditionally this is where the 'church' has come in. But not all churches meet this need, so you may simply have to watch out for fellow travellers on your way, and hold yourself open and willing to share with, and be supported by, them. Similarly, your spiritual journey, if it is to stay healthy, won't be kept separate from the rest of your life. It seems to be the case that you cannot grow in your knowledge of God and the things of God, without growing in awareness and knowledge of yourself. The two go hand in hand. And if you start to change, then that will gradually affect the whole of your life, not just one part of it.

But I haven't yet tried to explain what a meditation is, or how you might use a whole book of them. A meditation is a passage to be read slowly and thoughtfully, as a way into a deeper knowledge of God. We start then with some famous passages from the Bible because the Bible is the obvious place to start looking for Christian meditational material.

Now one way of describing the Bible is to see it as a peoples' collection, over many centuries, of the ways God has dealt with them. An amazing thing about this collection of sayings is that they have a capacity somehow to stay 'alive', and to continue to speak to us. Peoples' experience of God in the past is not so different from ours today. How God dealt with them, what God spoke to them, will often be recognized by us. They are not just 'dead' words from long ago.

The church's tradition of having readings from the Bible in church worship and, indeed, sermons drawing out the meaning of the words, together with the pattern of regular private Bible study, all witness to this way of thinking about the Bible. This is not to suggest that all passages will always speak to you. They won't. But some will. It might be that the passages that mean most to you are not included here: in which case why not draw up a list of your own? I am regularly delighted by the way people seem to go intuitively to the Bible passage they need, even if what it has to say to them comes as something of a surprise!

The Holy Spirit has spoken to, and through, many other men and women, beside those whose words are to be found in the Bible. So this book contains a taster of some of the other riches in the churches' tradition. Again, you will probably want to add words from other sources than those found here. Do see this little book as a starter pack, not as the finished article. The finished article you can only make for yourself. And you are not bound by the limitations of a book; there's no reason why you can't include music, and pictures, people and places in your finished article. Words aren't the only way in.

How to use these resources? My experience is that many people find it a help to have a regular time and place to meditate. Not to make you feel guilty if you miss it, but to help instil a sense of rhythm and discipline. Some discipline *is* required here: meditation can be fun, but it can also be very hard work. So what is the easiest time in the day to set aside ten or fifteen minutes? Maybe it's after a meal, or on the way to work, or when others have gone to bed. Choose a time that's easy. Wisdom says that sticking to a pattern like this is difficult for most of us, so find the easiest way into it that you can. Some are greatly helped by recognizing a holy place where they always sit, or perhaps walk. Maybe you have a corner of your home where your special things are, or a comfortable chair, or a favourite view. This might be the place to use.

Try to ensure a time of quiet, free from interruptions. So close the door, switch off the telephone. I regularly use a little alarm clock, set for whatever time I'm putting aside, so that I don't have to worry about time.

Then read the passage over slowly. People talk about chewing it over slowly, ruminating on it, a bit like a cow chewing grass! Let it mull around a while. The passage may have the capacity to speak on more than one level. Read it several times. Notice as you read, what thoughts and images come into your mind, and be prepared to follow them, see where they take you. It may be helpful to write down the thoughts that come, perhaps in the margin of the book (if it's yours) or in a special notebook. It doesn't matter how odd or unlikely the thoughts may be, write them down before you forget them. Often an insight will emerge over some days or even weeks, so if you don't record the clues as they come you may miss it.

Don't try and force the process. You don't have much control over all of this. All you can do is set aside some time and be attentive to what happens. A favourite saying of mine is, 'you can't push the river'. You will use up a lot of energy trying, but it won't achieve anything. You have to wait and go with the current. You don't really have a choice!

Expect most of the really valuable stuff to take place between your times of meditation, rather than during them. So you need to stay alert. Watch out for God reaching out to you through the ordinary events of your daily life. You might be helped by keeping a few minutes, before you read your passage, going back over the time since last you meditated. What's been happening in your life? Where might God have been reaching out to you?

People often want to pray when they have finished meditating: to talk to God about what they have been thinking or reflecting. This might be quite a long conversation, or a simple matter of offering something up to God, or perhaps just laying the time before God and being silent, listening and attentive. You might like to make a note of what you've prayed, to help you stay alert to God's answers. You may sometimes end your time of meditation with a commitment to do something.

Notice the number of 'mays' and 'mights' in all this. There is no one right way to meditate. There are no set rules, and no punishments for breaking them! Everybody will be a bit different. So do it in whatever way seems best to you, and stay willing to change as you learn something new, and as you grow. You may not be able to 'push the river', but it's astonishing how and where the river will take you if you let it. The key here, I think, is not to try and control what is happening. Rather, learn to trust that God is in control. In many ways learning that is all you need to do! Do try to find somebody, who knows a little bit more about it than you do, with whom you can share how you are getting on. Trying to do this 'solo' is not to be recommended.

In conclusion, may I record my thanks to those who've helped me pull this book together. My wife, Sylvia, gave much valued advice and bore with me through the gestation period, and my father, another Henry, and my eldest daughter Hannah, both drew my attention to pieces I didn't know, as did Ian Howarth, Paul Ferman and Sally Leeson, and Tony Lucas, good friends all of them. Thank you also to Alan, who has accompanied me on my journey for many years.

God bless this book to you,
Love, Joy, Peace and Hope,

Henry Morgan

JANUARY

Reflections from the Old Testament

✦ JANUARY 1 ✦

The Lord said to Abram, 'Leave your own country, your kin, and your father's house, and go to a country that I will show you. I shall make you into a great nation; I shall bless you and make your name so great that it will be used in blessings:

> those who bless you, I shall bless;
> those who curse you, I shall curse.
> All the peoples on earth
> will wish to be blessed as you are blessed.'

Abram, who was seventy-five years old when he left Harran, set out as the Lord had bidden him, and Lot went with him. He took his wife Sarai, his brother's son Lot, and all the possessions they had gathered and the dependants they had acquired in Harran, and they departed for Canaan. When they arrived there, Abram went on as far as the sanctuary at Shechem, the terebinth tree of Moreh.

Genesis 12:1–6

✦ JANUARY 2 ✦

The Lord appeared to Abraham by the oaks of Mamre, as he sat at the entrance of his tent in the heat of the day. He looked up and saw three men standing near him. When he saw them, he ran from the tent entrance to meet them, and bowed down to the ground.

He said, 'My lord, if I find favour with you, do not pass by your servant. Let a little water be brought, and wash your feet, and rest yourselves under the tree. Let me bring a little bread, that you may refresh yourselves, and after that you may pass on – since you have come to your servant.' So they said, 'Do as you have said.'

And Abraham hastened into the tent to Sarah, and said, 'Make ready quickly three measures of choice flour, knead it, and make cakes.' Abraham ran to the herd, and took a calf, tender and good, and gave it to the servant, who hastened to prepare it. Then he took curds and milk and the calf that he had prepared, and set it before them; and he stood by them under the tree while they ate.

❧ JANUARY 6 ❧

Then he said to Moses, 'Come up to the Lord, you and Aaron, Nadab, and Abihu, and seventy of the elders of Israel, and worship at a distance…

Then Moses and Aaron, Nadab, and Abihu, and seventy of the elders of Israel went up, and they saw the God of Israel. Under his feet there was something like a pavement of sapphire stone, like the very heaven for clearness. God did not lay his hand on the chief men of the people of Israel; also they beheld God, and they ate and drank.

Exodus 24:1, 9–11

❧ JANUARY 7 ❧

When the people saw that Moses delayed to come down from the mountain, the people gathered around Aaron and said to him, 'Come, make gods for us, who shall go before us; as for this Moses, the man who brought us up out of the land of Egypt, we do not know what has become of him.' Aaron said to them, 'Take off the gold rings that are on the ears of your wives, your sons, and your daughters, and bring them to me.'

So all the people took off the gold rings from their ears, and brought them to Aaron. He took the gold from them, formed it in a mould, and cast an image of a calf; and they said, 'These are your gods, O Israel, who brought you up out of the land of Egypt!' When Aaron saw this, he built an altar before it; and Aaron made proclamation and said, 'Tomorrow shall be a festival to the Lord.' They rose early the next day, and offered burnt offerings and brought sacrifices of well-being; and the people sat down to eat and drink, and rose up to revel.

The Lord said to Moses, 'Go down at once! Your people, whom you brought up out of the land of Egypt, have acted perversely; they have been quick to turn aside from the way that I commanded them; they have cast for themselves an image of a calf, and have worshipped it and sacrificed to it, and said, "These are your gods, O Israel, who brought you up out of the land of Egypt!"'

Exodus 32:1–8

❧ JANUARY 8 ❧

In this year of jubilee you shall return, every one of you, to your property. When you make a sale to your neighbour or buy from your neighbour, you shall not cheat one another. When you buy from your neighbour, you shall pay only for the number of years since the jubilee; the seller shall charge you only for the remaining crop years. If the years are more, you shall increase the price, and if the years are fewer, you shall diminish the price; for it is a certain number of harvests that are being sold to you. You shall not cheat one another, but you shall fear your God; for I am the Lord your God.

You shall observe my statutes and faithfully keep my ordinances, so that you may live on the land securely. The land will yield its fruit, and you will eat your fill and live on it securely. Should you ask, 'What shall we eat in the seventh year, if we may not sow or gather in our crop?' I will order my blessing for you in the sixth year, so that it will yield a crop for three years. When you sow in the eighth year, you will be eating from the old crop; until the ninth year, when its produce comes in, you shall eat the old.

Leviticus 25:13–22

❧ JANUARY 9 ❧

Now there was no water for the congregation; so they gathered together against Moses and against Aaron. The people quarrelled with Moses and said, 'Would that we had died when our kindred died before the Lord! Why have you brought the assembly of the Lord into this wilderness for us and our livestock to die here? Why have you brought us up out of Egypt, to bring us to this wretched place? It is no place for grain, or figs, or vines, or pomegranates; and there is no water to drink.'

Then Moses and Aaron went away from the assembly to the entrance of the tent of meeting; they fell on their faces, and the glory of the Lord appeared to them. The Lord spoke to Moses, saying: 'Take the staff, and assemble the congregation, you and your brother Aaron, and command the rock before their eyes to yield its water. Thus you shall bring water out of the rock for them; thus you shall provide drink for the congregation and their livestock.'

But the Lord said to Moses and Aaron, 'Because you did not trust in me, to show my holiness before the eyes of the Israelites, therefore you shall not bring this assembly into the land that I have given them.'

Numbers 20:2–8, 12

❧ JANUARY 10 ❧

Now the boy Samuel was ministering to the Lord under Eli. The word of the Lord was rare in those days; visions were not widespread.

At that time Eli, whose eyesight had begun to grow dim so that he could not see, was lying down in his room; the lamp of God had not yet gone out, and Samuel was lying down in the temple of the Lord, where the ark of God was. Then the Lord called, 'Samuel! Samuel!' and he said, 'Here I am!' and ran to Eli, and said, 'Here I am, for you called me.' But he said, 'I did not call; lie down again.' So he went and lay down. The Lord called again, 'Samuel!' Samuel got up and went to Eli, and said, 'Here I am, for you called me.' But he said, 'I did not call, my son; lie down again.' Now Samuel did not yet know the Lord, and the word of the Lord had not yet been revealed to him. The Lord called Samuel again, a third time. And he got up and went to Eli, and said, 'Here I am, for you called me.' Then Eli perceived that the Lord was calling the boy. Therefore Eli said to Samuel, 'Go, lie down; and if he calls you, you shall say, "Speak, Lord, for your servant is listening."' So Samuel went and lay down in his place.

Now the Lord came and stood there, calling as before, 'Samuel! Samuel!' And Samuel said, 'Speak, for your servant is listening.' Then the Lord said to Samuel, 'See, I am about to do something in Israel that will make both ears of anyone who hears of it tingle. On that day I will fulfil against Eli all that I have spoken concerning his house, from beginning to end. For I have told him that I am about to punish his house for ever, for the iniquity that he knew, because his sons were blaspheming God, and he did not restrain them. Therefore I swear to the house of Eli that the iniquity of Eli's house shall not be expiated by sacrifice or offering for ever.'

Samuel lay there until morning; then he opened the doors of the house of the Lord. Samuel was afraid to tell the vision to Eli. But Eli called Samuel and said, 'Samuel, my son.' He said, 'Here I am.' Eli said,

'What was it that he told you? Do not hide it from me. May God do so to you and more also, if you hide anything from me of all that he told you.' So Samuel told him everything and hid nothing from him. Then he said, 'It is the Lord; let him do what seems good to him.'

1 Samuel 3:1–18

❧ JANUARY 11 ❧

At Gibeon the Lord appeared to Solomon in a dream by night; and God said, 'Ask what I should give you.' And Solomon said, 'You have shown great and steadfast love to your servant my father David, because he walked before you in faithfulness, in righteousness, and in uprightness of heart towards you; and you have kept for him this great and steadfast love, and have given him a son to sit on his throne today. And now, O Lord my God, you have made your servant king in place of my father David, although I am only a little child; I do not know how to go out or come in. And your servant is in the midst of the people whom you have chosen, a great people, so numerous they cannot be numbered or counted. Give your servant therefore an understanding mind to govern your people, able to discern between good and evil; for who can govern this your great people?'

It pleased the Lord that Solomon had asked this. God said to him, 'Because you have asked this, and have not asked for yourself long life or riches, or for the life of your enemies, but have asked for yourself understanding to discern what is right, I now do according to your word. Indeed I give you a wise and discerning mind; no one like you has been before you and no one like you shall arise after you. I give you also what you have not asked, both riches and honour all your life; no other king shall compare with you. If you will walk in my ways, keeping my statutes and my commandments, as your father David walked, then I will lengthen your life.'

Then Solomon awoke; it had been a dream. He came to Jerusalem where he stood before the ark of the covenant of the Lord. He offered up burnt-offerings and offerings of well-being, and provided a feast for all his servants.

1 Kings 3:5–15

Ahab told Jezebel all that Elijah had done, and how he had killed all the prophets with the sword. Then Jezebel sent a messenger to Elijah, saying, 'So may the gods do to me, and more also, if I do not make your life like the life of one of them by this time tomorrow.' Then he was afraid; he got up and fled for his life, and came to Beer-sheba, which belongs to Judah; he left his servant there.

But he himself went a day's journey into the wilderness, and came and sat down under a solitary broom tree. He asked that he might die: 'It is enough; now, O Lord, take away my life, for I am no better than my ancestors.' Then he lay down under the broom tree and fell asleep. Suddenly an angel touched him and said to him, 'Get up and eat.' He looked, and there at his head was a cake baked on hot stones, and a jar of water. He ate and drank, and lay down again. The angel of the Lord came a second time, touched him, and said, 'Get up and eat, otherwise the journey will be too much for you.' He got up, and ate and drank; then he went in the strength of that food for forty days and forty nights to Horeb the mount of God. At that place he came to a cave, and spent the night there.

Then the word of the Lord came to him, saying, 'What are you doing here, Elijah?' He answered, 'I have been very zealous for the Lord, the God of hosts; for the Israelites have forsaken your covenant, thrown down your altars, and killed your prophets with the sword. I alone am left, and they are seeking my life, to take it away.'

He said, 'Go out and stand on the mountain before the Lord, for the Lord is about to pass by.' Now there was a great wind, so strong that it was splitting mountains and breaking rocks in pieces before the Lord, but the Lord was not in the wind; and after the wind an earthquake, but the Lord was not in the earthquake; and after the earthquake a fire, but the Lord was not in the fire; and after the fire a sound of sheer silence.

1 Kings 19:1–12

🌀 JANUARY 13 🌸

Once when the king of Aram was at war with Israel, he took counsel with his officers. He said, 'At such and such a place shall be my camp.'

But the man of God sent word to the king of Israel, 'Take care not to pass this place, because the Aramaeans are going down there.' The king of Israel sent word to the place of which the man of God spoke. More than once or twice he warned such a place so that it was on the alert.

The mind of the king of Aram was greatly perturbed because of this; he called his officers and said to them, 'Now tell me who among us sides with the king of Israel?' Then one of his officers said, 'No one, my lord king. It is Elisha, the prophet in Israel, who tells the king of Israel the words that you speak in your bedchamber.' He said, 'Go and find where he is; I will send and seize him.' He was told, 'He is in Dothan.' So he sent horses and chariots there and a great army; they came by night, and surrounded the city.

When an attendant of the man of God rose early in the morning and went out, an army with horses and chariots was all around the city. His servant said, 'Alas, master! What shall we do?' He replied, 'Do not be afraid, for there are more with us than there are with them.' Then Elisha prayed: 'O Lord, please open his eyes that he may see.' So the Lord opened the eyes of the servant, and he saw; the mountain was full of horses and chariots of fire all around Elisha.

2 Kings 6:8–17

❧ JANUARY 14 ❧

One day the heavenly beings came to present themselves before the Lord, and Satan also came among them to present himself before the Lord. The Lord said to Satan, 'Where have you come from?' Satan answered the Lord, 'From going to and fro on the earth, and from walking up and down on it.' The Lord said to Satan, 'Have you considered my servant Job? There is no one like him on the earth, a blameless and upright man who fears God and turns away from evil. He still persists in his integrity, although you incited me against him, to destroy him for no reason.' Then Satan answered the Lord, 'Skin for skin! All that people have they will give to save their lives. But stretch out your hand now and touch his bone and his flesh, and he will curse you to your face.' The Lord said to Satan, 'Very well, he is in your power; only spare his life.'

So Satan went out from the presence of the Lord, and inflicted loathsome sores on Job from the sole of his foot to the crown of his head. Job took a potsherd with which to scrape himself, and sat among the ashes.

Then his wife said to him, 'Do you still persist in your integrity? Curse God, and die.' But he said to her, 'You speak as any foolish woman would speak. Shall we receive the good at the hand of God, and not receive the bad?' In all this Job did not sin with his lips.

Job 2:1–10

🐚 JANUARY 15 🐚

They have gaped at me with their mouths;
    they have struck me insolently on the cheek;
    they mass themselves together against me.
God gives me up to the ungodly,
    and casts me into the hands of the wicked.
I was at ease, and he broke me in two;
    he seized me by the neck and dashed me to pieces;
he set me up as his target;
    his archers surround me.
He slashes open my kidneys, and shows no mercy;
    he pours out my gall on the ground.
He bursts upon me again and again;
    he rushes at me like a warrior.
I have sewed sackcloth upon my skin,
    and have laid my strength in the dust.
My face is red with weeping,
    and deep darkness is on my eyelids,
though there is no violence in my hands,
    and my prayer is pure.

O earth, do not cover my blood;
    let my outcry find no resting place.
Even now, in fact, my witness is in heaven,
    and he that vouches for me is on high.

My friends scorn me;
 my eye pours out tears to God,
that he would maintain the right of a mortal with God,
 as one does for a neighbour.
For when a few years have come,
 I shall go the way from which I shall not return.

Job 16:10–22

🦋 JANUARY 16 🦋

Trust in the Lord with all your heart,
 and do not rely on your own insight.
In all your ways acknowledge him,
 and he will make straight your paths.
Do not be wise in your own eyes;
 fear the Lord, and turn away from evil.
It will be a healing for your flesh
 and a refreshment for your body.

Honour the Lord with your substance
 and with the first fruits of all your produce;
then your barns will be filled with plenty,
 and your vats will be bursting with wine.

My child, do not despise the Lord's discipline
 or be weary of his reproof,
for the Lord reproves the one he loves,
 as a father the son in whom he delights.

Proverbs 3:5–12

🦋 JANUARY 17 🦋

For everything there is a season, and a time for every matter under heaven:
 a time to be born, and a time to die;
 a time to plant, and a time to pluck up what is planted;

a time to kill, and a time to heal;
a time to break down, and a time to build up;
a time to weep, and a time to laugh;
a time to mourn, and a time to dance;
a time to throw away stones, and a time to gather stones together;
a time to embrace, and a time to refrain from embracing;
a time to seek, and a time to lose;
a time to keep, and a time to throw away;
a time to tear, and a time to sew;
a time to keep silence, and a time to speak;
a time to love, and a time to hate;
a time for war, and a time for peace.

Ecclesiastes 3:1–8

❦ JANUARY 18 ❦

The voice of my beloved!
    Look, he comes,
leaping upon the mountains,
    bounding over the hills.
My beloved is like a gazelle
    or a young stag.
Look, there he stands
    behind our wall,
gazing in at the windows,
    looking through the lattice.
My beloved speaks and says to me:

'Arise, my love, my fair one,
    and come away;
for now the winter is past,
    the rain is over and gone.
The flowers appear on the earth;
    the time of singing has come,
and the voice of the turtledove
    is heard in our land.

The fig tree puts forth its figs,
    and the vines are in blossom;
    they give forth fragrance.
Arise, my love, my fair one,
    and come away.'

Song of Solomon 2:8–13

❧ JANUARY 19 ❧

My beloved thrust his hand into the opening,
    and my inmost being yearned for him.
I arose to open to my beloved,
    and my hands dripped with myrrh,
my fingers with liquid myrrh,
    upon the handles of the bolt.
I opened to my beloved,
    but my beloved had turned and was gone.
My soul failed me when he spoke.
I sought him, but did not find him;
    I called him, but he gave no answer.
Making their rounds in the city
    the sentinels found me;
they beat me, they wounded me,
    they took away my mantle,
    those sentinels of the walls.
I adjure you, O daughters of Jerusalem,
    if you find my beloved,
tell him this:
    I am faint with love.

Song of Solomon 5:4–8

❧ JANUARY 20 ❧

Deal bountifully with your servant,
    so that I may live and observe your word.

Open my eyes, so that I may behold
   wondrous things out of your law.
I live as an alien in the land;
   do not hide your commandments from me.
My soul is consumed with longing
   for your ordinances at all times.
You rebuke the insolent, accursed ones,
   who wander from your commandments;
take away from me their scorn and contempt,
   for I have kept your decrees.
Even though princes sit plotting against me,
   your servant will meditate on your statutes.
Your decrees are my delight,
   they are my counsellors.

Psalm 119:17–24

❧ JANUARY 21 ❧

Refrain: Always aware of us,
ever-present with us
ceaselessly creating us –
we respond in love,
we tremble and adore,
our God, mysterious and faithful.

Light of light, you have searched me out and known me.
You know where I am, and where I go,
you see my thoughts from afar.
You discern my paths and my resting places,
you are acquainted with all my ways.
Yes, and not a word comes from my lips
but you, O God, have heard it already.
You are in front of me and you are behind me,
you have laid your hand on my shoulder.
Such knowledge is too wonderful for me,
so great that I cannot fathom it.

Where shall I go from your Spirit,
where shall I flee from your Presence?
If I climb to the heavens you are there:
if I descend to the depths of the earth, you are there also.
If I spread my wings towards the morning,
and fly to the uttermost shores of the sea,
even there your hand will lead me,
and your right hand will hold me.
If I should cry to the darkness to cover me,
and the night to enclose me,
the darkness is no darkness to you,
and the night is as clear as the day.

For you have created every part of my being,
cell and tissue, blood and bone.
You have woven me in the womb of my mother;
I will praise you, so wonderfully am I made.
Awesome are your deeds and marvellous are your works.
You know me to the very core of my being;
Nothing in me was hidden from your eyes
when I was formed in silence and secrecy,
in intricate splendour in the depths of the earth.
Even as they were forming you saw my limbs,
each part of my body shaped by your finger.

How deep are your thoughts to me, O God,
how great is the sum of them.
Were I to count them they are more in number
than the grains of sand upon the sea-shore...
and still I would know nothing about you...
yet still would you hold me in the palm of your hand.

Yet my trust falters. I see all that is wrong in the world and in my heart,
all the mutual loathing and hatreds, all the betrayals and lies.
Scour our hearts, refine our thoughts, strengthen our wills,
guide us in your Way.

Psalm 139, rephrased by Jim Cotter

JANUARY 22

In the year that King Uzziah died, I saw the Lord sitting on a throne, high and lofty; and the hem of his robe filled the temple. Seraphs were in attendance above him; each had six wings: with two they covered their faces, and with two they covered their feet, and with two they flew. And one called to another and said:

'Holy, holy, holy is the Lord of hosts;
the whole earth is full of his glory.'

The pivots on the thresholds shook at the voices of those who called, and the house filled with smoke. And I said: 'Woe is me! I am lost, for I am a man of unclean lips, and I live among a people of unclean lips; yet my eyes have seen the King, the Lord of hosts!'

Then one of the seraphs flew to me, holding a live coal that had been taken from the altar with a pair of tongs. The seraph touched my mouth with it and said: 'Now that this has touched your lips, your guilt has departed and your sin is blotted out.' Then I heard the voice of the Lord saying, 'Whom shall I send, and who will go for us?' And I said, 'Here am I; send me!'

Isaiah 6:1–8

JANUARY 23

Comfort, O comfort my people,
   says your God.
Speak tenderly to Jerusalem,
   and cry to her
that she has served her term,
   that her penalty is paid,
that she has received from the Lord's hand
   double for all her sins.

A voice cries out:
'In the wilderness prepare the way of the Lord,
   make straight in the desert a highway for our God.

Every valley shall be lifted up,
      and every mountain and hill be made low;
the uneven ground shall become level,
      and the rough places a plain.
Then the glory of the Lord shall be revealed,
      and all people shall see it together,
for the mouth of the Lord has spoken.'

A voice says, 'Cry out!'
      And I said, 'What shall I cry?'
All people are grass,
      their constancy is like the flower of the field.
The grass withers, the flower fades,
      when the breath of the Lord blows upon it;
      surely the people are grass.
The grass withers, the flower fades;
      but the word of our God will stand for ever.

Isaiah 40:1–8

🌸 JANUARY 24 🌸

See, my servant shall prosper;
      he shall be exalted and lifted up,
      and shall be very high.
Just as there were many who were astonished at him
      – so marred was his appearance,
            beyond human semblance,
      and his form beyond that of mortals –
so he shall startle many nations;
      kings shall shut their mouths because of him;
for that which had not been told them they shall see,
      and that which they had not heard they shall contemplate.
Who has believed what we have heard?
      And to whom has the arm of the Lord been revealed?
For he grew up before him like a young plant,
      and like a root out of dry ground;

he had no form or majesty that we should look at him,
    nothing in his appearance that we should desire him.
He was despised and rejected by others;
    a man of suffering and acquainted with infirmity;
and as one from whom others hide their faces
    he was despised, and we held him of no account.

Surely he has borne our infirmities
    and carried our diseases;
yet we accounted him stricken,
    struck down by God, and afflicted.
But he was wounded for our transgressions,
    crushed for our iniquities;
upon him was the punishment that made us whole,
    and by his bruises we are healed.
All we like sheep have gone astray;
    we have all turned to our own way,
and the Lord has laid on him
    the iniquity of us all.

He was oppressed, and he was afflicted,
    yet he did not open his mouth;
like a lamb that is led to the slaughter,
    and like a sheep that before its shearers is silent,
    so he did not open his mouth.
By a perversion of justice he was taken away.
    Who could have imagined his future?
For he was cut off from the land of the living,
    stricken for the transgression of my people.
They made his grave with the wicked
    and his tomb with the rich,
although he had done no violence,
    and there was no deceit in his mouth.

Yet it was the will of the Lord to crush him with pain.
When you make his life an offering for sin,
    he shall see his offspring, and shall prolong his days;
through him the will of the Lord shall prosper.
    Out of his anguish he shall see light;

he shall find satisfaction through his knowledge.

> The righteous one, my servant,
>   shall make many righteous,
> and he shall bear their iniquities.

Therefore I will allot him a portion with the great,
    and he shall divide the spoil with the strong;
because he poured out himself to death,
    and was numbered with the transgressors;
yet he bore the sin of many,
    and made intercession for the transgressors.

Isaiah 52:13 – 53:12

❦ JANUARY 25 ❦

Now the word of the Lord came to me saying,

> 'Before I formed you in the womb I knew you,
> and before you were born I consecrated you;
> I appointed you a prophet to the nations.'

Then I said, 'Ah, Lord God! Truly I do not know how to speak, for I am only a boy.' But the Lord said to me,

> 'Do not say, "I am only a boy";
> for you shall go to all to whom I send you,
> and you shall speak whatever I command you,
> Do not be afraid of them,
> for I am with you to deliver you,' says the Lord.

Then the Lord put out his hand and touched my mouth; and the Lord said to me,

> 'Now I have put my words in your mouth.
> See, today I appoint you over nations and over kingdoms,
> to pluck up and to pull down,
> to destroy and to overthrow,
> to build and to plant.'

Jeremiah 1:4–10

O Lord, you have enticed me,
     and I was enticed;
you have overpowered me,
     and you have prevailed.
I have become a laughing-stock all day long;
     everyone mocks me...

Cursed be the day
     on which I was born!
The day when my mother bore me,
     let it not be blessed!
Cursed be the man
     who brought the news to my father,
                    saying,
'A child is born to you, a son,'
     making him very glad.
Let that man be like the cities
     that the Lord overthrew without pity;
let him hear a cry in the morning
     and an alarm at noon,
because he did not kill me in the womb;
     so my mother would have been my grave,
     and her womb for ever great.
Why did I come forth from the womb
     to see toil and sorrow,
     and spend my days in shame?

Jeremiah 20:7, 14–18

JANUARY 27

The days are surely coming, says the Lord, when I will make a new
covenant with the house of Israel and the house of Judah. It will not
be like the covenant that I made with their ancestors when I took
them by the hand to bring them out of the land of Egypt – a covenant

that they broke, though I was their husband, says the Lord. But this is the covenant that I will make with the house of Israel after those days, says the Lord: I will put my law within them, and I will write it on their hearts; and I will be their God, and they shall be my people. No longer shall they teach one another, or say to each other, 'Know the Lord', for they shall all know me, from the least of them to the greatest, says the Lord; for I will forgive their iniquity, and remember their sin no more.

Jeremiah 31:31–34

JANUARY 28

The hand of the Lord came upon me, and he brought me out by the spirit of the Lord and set me down in the middle of a valley; it was full of bones. He led me all round them; there were very many lying in the valley, and they were very dry. He said to me, 'Mortal, can these bones live?' I answered, 'O Lord God, you know.' Then he said to me, 'Prophesy to these bones, and say to them: O dry bones, hear the word of the Lord. Thus says the Lord God to these bones: I will cause breath to enter you, and you shall live. I will lay sinews on you, and will cause flesh to come upon you, and cover you with skin, and put breath in you, and you shall live; and you shall know that I am the Lord.'

So I prophesied as I had been commanded; and as I prophesied, suddenly there was a noise, a rattling, and the bones came together, bone to its bone. I looked, and there were sinews on them, and flesh had come upon them, and skin had covered them; but there was no breath in them. Then he said to me, 'Prophesy to the breath, prophesy, mortal, and say to the breath: Thus says the Lord God: Come from the four winds, O breath, and breathe upon these slain, that they may live.' I prophesied as he commanded me, and the breath came into them, and they lived, and stood on their feet, a vast multitude.

Then he said to me, 'Mortal, these bones are the whole house of Israel. They say, "Our bones are dried up, and our hope is lost; we are cut off completely." Therefore prophesy, and say to them, Thus says the Lord God: I am going to open your graves, and bring you up from your graves, O my people; and I will bring you back to the land of Israel. And you shall know that I am the Lord, when I open your graves, and bring you up from your graves, O my people. I will put my spirit within you, and you shall live, and I will place you on your own soil; then you shall know that I, the Lord, have spoken and will act,' says the Lord.

Ezekiel 37:1–14

❧ JANUARY 29 ❧

This is what the Lord God showed me: he was forming locusts at the time the latter growth began to sprout (it was the latter growth after the king's mowings). When they had finished eating the grass of the land, I said,

'O Lord God, forgive, I beg you!
　　How can Jacob stand?
　　He is so small!'

The Lord relented concerning this;

'It shall not be,' said the Lord...

This is what he showed me: the Lord was standing beside a wall built with a plumb-line, with a plumb-line in his hand. And the Lord said to me, 'Amos, what do you see?' And I said, 'A plumb-line.' Then the Lord said,

'See, I am setting a plumb-line
　　in the midst of my people Israel;
　　I will never again pass them by;
the high places of Isaac shall be made desolate,
　　and the sanctuaries of Israel shall be laid waste,
　　and I will rise against the house of Jeroboam with the sword'...

This is what the Lord God showed me – a basket of summer fruit. He said, 'Amos, what do you see?' And I said, 'A basket of summer fruit.' Then the Lord said to me,

'The end has come upon my people Israel;
　　I will never again pass them by.

The songs of the temple shall become wailings on that day,'
        says the Lord God;
'the dead bodies shall be many,
        cast out in every place. Be silent!'

Amos 7:1–3, 7–9; 8:1–3

JANUARY 30

He has told you, O mortal, what is good;
        and what does the Lord require of you
but to do justice, and to love kindness,
        and to walk humbly with your God?

Micah 6:8

JANUARY 31

I will stand at my watchpost,
        and station myself on the rampart;
I will keep watch to see what he will say to me,
        and what he will answer concerning my complaint.
Then the Lord answered me and said:

Write the vision;
        make it plain on tablets,
        so that a runner may read it.
For there is still a vision for the appointed time;
        it speaks of the end, and does not lie.
If it seems to tarry, wait for it;
        it will surely come, it will not delay.

Habakkuk 2:1–3

FEBRUARY

Reflections from the New Testament

❧ FEBRUARY 1 ❧

In the beginning was the Word, and the Word was with God, and the Word was God. The same was in the beginning with God. All things were made by him; and without him was not any thing made that was made. In him was life; and the life was the light of men. And the light shineth in darkness; and the darkness comprehended it not.

There was a man sent from God, whose name was John. The same came for a witness, to bear witness of the Light, that all men through him might believe. He was not that Light, but was sent to bear witness of that Light. That was the true Light, which lighteth every man that cometh into the world. He was in the world, and the world was made by him, and the world knew him not. He came unto his own, and his own received him not.

But as many as received him, to them gave he power to become the sons of God, even to them that believe on his name: which were born, not of blood, nor of the will of the flesh, nor of the will of man, but of God.

And the Word was made flesh, and dwelt among us, (and we beheld his glory, the glory as of the only begotten of the Father,) full of grace and truth.

John 1:1–14

❧ FEBRUARY 2 ❧

In the sixth month the angel Gabriel was sent by God to a town in Galilee called Nazareth, to a virgin engaged to a man whose name was Joseph, of the house of David. The virgin's name was Mary. And he came to her and said, 'Greetings, favoured one! The Lord is with you.' But she was much perplexed by his words and pondered what sort of greeting this might be. The angel said to her, 'Do not be afraid, Mary, for you have found favour with God. And now, you will conceive in your womb and bear a son, and you will name him Jesus. He will be great, and will be called the Son of the Most High, and the Lord God will give to him the throne of his ancestor David. He will reign over the house of Jacob for ever, and of his kingdom there will be no end.' Mary said to the angel, 'How can this be, since I am a virgin?' The angel said to her,

'The Holy Spirit will come upon you, and the power of the Most High will overshadow you; therefore the child to be born will be holy; he will be called Son of God. And now, your relative Elizabeth in her old age has also conceived a son; and this is the sixth month for her who was said to be barren. For nothing will be impossible with God.' Then Mary said, 'Here am I, the servant of the Lord; let it be with me according to your word.' Then the angel departed from her.

Luke 1:26–38

✦ FEBRUARY 3 ✦

Now when all the people were baptized, and when Jesus also had been baptized and was praying, the heaven was opened, and the Holy Spirit descended upon him in bodily form like a dove. And a voice came from heaven, 'You are my Son, the Beloved; with you I am well pleased.' Jesus was about thirty years old when he began his work. He was the son (as was thought) of Joseph son of Heli...

Luke 3:21–23

✦ FEBRUARY 4 ✦

Jesus, full of the Holy Spirit, returned from the Jordan and was led by the Spirit in the wilderness, where for forty days he was tempted by the devil. He ate nothing at all during those days, and when they were over, he was famished. The devil said to him, 'If you are the Son of God, command this stone to become a loaf of bread.' Jesus answered him, 'It is written, "One does not live by bread alone."'

Then the devil led him up and showed him in an instant all the kingdoms of the world. And the devil said to him, 'To you I will give their glory and all this authority; for it has been given over to me, and I give it to anyone I please. If you, then, will worship me, it will all be yours.' Jesus answered him, 'It is written,

"Worship the Lord your God,
    and serve only him."'

Then the devil took him to Jerusalem, and placed him on the pinnacle of the temple, saying to him, 'If you are the Son of God, throw yourself down from here, for it is written,

"He will command his angels concerning you,
    to protect you,"

and

"On their hands they will bear you up,
    so that you will not dash your foot against a stone."'

Jesus answered him, 'It is said, "Do not put the Lord your God to the test."' When the devil had finished every test, he departed from him until an opportune time.

Luke 4:1–13

❧ FEBRUARY 5 ❧

Nicodemus said to him, 'How can anyone be born after having grown old? Can one enter a second time into the mother's womb and be born?' Jesus answered, 'Very truly, I tell you, no one can enter the kingdom of God without being born of water and Spirit. What is born of the flesh is flesh, and what is born of the Spirit is spirit. Do not be astonished that I said to you, 'You must be born from above.' The wind blows where it chooses, and you hear the sound of it, but you do not know where it comes from or where it goes. So it is with everyone who is born of the Spirit.'

John 3:4–8

❧ FEBRUARY 6 ❧

A Samaritan woman came to draw water, and Jesus said to her, 'Give me a drink.' (His disciples had gone to the city to buy food.) The Samaritan woman said to him, 'How is it that you, a Jew, ask a drink of me, a woman of Samaria?' (Jews do not share things in common with Samaritans.) Jesus answered her, 'If you knew the gift of God, and who it is that is saying to you, "Give me a drink," you would have asked him, and he would have given you living water.' The woman said to him, 'Sir, you have no bucket, and the well is deep. Where do you get that living water? Are you greater than our ancestor Jacob, who gave us the well, and with his sons and his flocks drank from it?' Jesus said to her, 'Everyone who drinks of this water will be thirsty again, but those who drink of the water that I will give them will never be thirsty. The water that I will give will become in them a spring of water gushing up to eternal life.' The woman said to him, 'Sir, give me this water, so that I may never be thirsty or have to keep coming here to draw water.'

Jesus said to her, 'Go, call your husband, and come back.' The woman answered him, 'I have no husband.' Jesus said to her, 'You are right in saying, "I have no husband"; for you have had five husbands, and the one you have now is not your husband. What you have said is true!' The woman said to him, 'Sir, I see that you are a prophet. Our ancestors worshipped on this mountain, but you say that the place where people must worship is in Jerusalem.' Jesus said to her, 'Woman, believe me, the hour is coming when you will worship the Father neither on this mountain nor in Jerusalem. You worship what you do not know; we worship what we know, for salvation is from the Jews. But the hour is coming, and is now here, when the true worshippers will worship the Father in spirit and truth, for the Father seeks such as these to worship him. God is spirit, and those who worship him must worship in spirit and truth.' The woman said to him, 'I know that Messiah is coming' (who is called Christ). 'When he comes, he will proclaim all things to us.' Jesus said to her, 'I am he, the one who is speaking to you.'

John 4:7–26

❦ FEBRUARY 7 ❦

Then Jesus said to them, 'Very truly, I tell you, it was not Moses who gave you the bread from heaven, but it is my Father who gives you the true bread from heaven. For the bread of God is that which comes down from heaven and gives life to the world.' They said to him, 'Sir, give us this bread always.'

Jesus said to them, 'I am the bread of life. Whoever comes to me will never be hungry, and whoever believes in me will never be thirsty.'

John 6:32–35

❧ FEBRUARY 8 ☙

'You are the salt of the earth; but if salt has lost its taste, how can its saltiness be restored? It is no longer good for anything, but is thrown out and trampled under foot.

'You are the light of the world. A city built on a hill cannot be hidden. No one after lighting a lamp puts it under the bushel basket, but on the lampstand, and it gives light to all in the house. In the same way, let your light shine before others, so that they may see your good works and give glory to your Father in heaven.'

Matthew 5:13–16

❧ FEBRUARY 9 ☙

'Beware of practising your piety before others in order to be seen by them; for then you have no reward from your Father in heaven.

'So whenever you give alms, do not sound a trumpet before you, as the hypocrites do in the synagogues and in the streets, so that they may be praised by others. Truly I tell you, they have received their reward. But when you give alms, do not let your left hand know what your right hand is doing, so that your alms may be done in secret; and your Father who sees in secret will reward you.

'And whenever you pray, do not be like the hypocrites; for they love to stand and pray in the synagogues and at the street corners, so that they may be seen by others. Truly I tell you, they have received their reward. But whenever you pray, go into your room and shut the door and pray to your Father who is in secret; and your Father who sees in secret will reward you.

'When you are praying, do not heap up empty phrases as the Gentiles do; for they think that they will be heard because of their many words.

Do not be like them, for your Father knows what you need before you ask him.'

Matthew 6:1–8

❦ FEBRUARY 10 ❦

'So I say to you, Ask, and it will be given to you; search, and you will find; knock, and the door will be opened for you. For everyone who asks receives, and everyone who searches finds, and for everyone who knocks, the door will be opened. Is there anyone among you who, if your child asks for a fish, will give a snake instead of a fish? Or if the child asks for an egg, will give a scorpion? If you then, who are evil, know how to give good gifts to your children, how much more will the heavenly Father give the Holy Spirit to those who ask him!'

Luke 11:9–13

❦ FEBRUARY 11 ❦

Just then there came a man named Jairus, a leader of the synagogue. He fell at Jesus' feet and begged him to come to his house, for he had an only daughter, about twelve years old, who was dying.

As he went, the crowds pressed in on him. Now there was a woman who had been suffering from haemorrhages for twelve years; and though she had spent all she had on physicians, no one could cure her. She came up behind him and touched the fringe of his clothes, and immediately her haemorrhage stopped. Then Jesus asked, 'Who touched me?' When all denied it, Peter said, 'Master, the crowds surround you and press in on you.' But Jesus said, 'Someone touched me; for I noticed that power had gone out from me.' When the woman saw that she could not remain hidden, she came trembling; and falling down before him, she declared in the presence of all the people why she had touched him, and how she had been immediately healed. He said to her, 'Daughter, your faith has made you well; go in peace.'

While he was still speaking, someone came from the leader's house to say, 'Your daughter is dead; do not trouble the teacher any longer.' When Jesus heard this, he replied, 'Do not fear. Only believe, and she will be saved.' When he came to the house, he did not allow anyone to enter with him, except Peter, John, and James, and the child's father and mother. They were all weeping and wailing for her; but he said, 'Do not weep; for she is not dead but sleeping.' And they laughed at him, knowing that she was dead. But he took her by the hand and called out, 'Child, get up!' Her spirit returned, and she got up at once. Then he directed them to give her something to eat. Her parents were astounded; but he ordered them to tell no one what had happened.

Luke 8:41–56

❧ FEBRUARY 12 ❧

Then he said to them all, 'If any want to become my followers, let them deny themselves and take up their cross daily and follow me. For those who want to save their life will lose it, and those who lose their life for my sake will save it. What does it profit them if they gain the whole world, but lose or forfeit themselves? Those who are ashamed of me and of my words, of them the Son of Man will be ashamed when he comes in his glory and the glory of the Father and of the holy angels. But truly I tell you, there are some standing here who will not taste death before they see the kingdom of God.'

Now about eight days after these sayings Jesus took with him Peter and John and James, and went up on the mountain to pray. And while he was praying, the appearance of his face changed, and his clothes became dazzling white. Suddenly they saw two men, Moses and Elijah, talking to him. They appeared in glory and were speaking of his departure, which he was about to accomplish at Jerusalem. Now Peter and his companions were weighed down with sleep; but since they had stayed awake, they saw his glory and the two men who stood with him. Just as they were leaving him, Peter said to Jesus, 'Master, it is good for us to be here; let us make three dwellings, one for you, one for Moses, and one for Elijah' – not knowing what he said. While he was saying this, a cloud came and overshadowed them; and they were terrified as they entered the cloud. Then from the cloud came a voice that said,

'This is my Son, my Chosen; listen to him!' When the voice had spoken, Jesus was found alone. And they kept silent and in those days told no one any of the things they had seen.

Luke 9:23–36

FEBRUARY 13

Now as they went on their way, he entered a certain village, where a woman named Martha welcomed him into her home. She had a sister named Mary, who sat at the Lord's feet and listened to what he was saying. But Martha was distracted by her many tasks; so she came to him and asked, 'Lord, do you not care that my sister has left me to do all the work by myself? Tell her then to help me.' But the Lord answered her, 'Martha, Martha, you are worried and distracted by many things; there is need of only one thing. Mary has chosen the better part, which will not be taken away from her.'

Luke 10:38–42

FEBRUARY 14

Jesus, knowing that the Father had given all things into his hands, and that he had come from God and was going to God, got up from the table, took off his outer robe, and tied a towel around himself. Then he poured water into a basin and began to wash the disciples' feet and to wipe them with the towel that was tied around him. He came to Simon Peter, who said to him, 'Lord, are you going to wash my feet?' Jesus answered, 'You do not know now what I am doing, but later you will understand.' Peter said to him, 'You will never wash my feet.' Jesus answered, 'Unless I wash you, you have no share with me.' Simon Peter said to him, 'Lord, not my feet only but also my hands and my head!' Jesus said to him, 'One who has bathed does not need to wash, except for the feet, but is entirely clean. And you are clean, though not all of you.' For he knew who was to betray him; for this reason he said, 'Not all of you are clean.'

After he had washed their feet, had put on his robe, and had returned to the table, he said to them, 'Do you know what I have done to you? You call me Teacher and Lord – and you are right, for that is what I am. So if I, your Lord and Teacher, have washed your feet, you also ought to wash one another's feet. For I have set you an example, that you also should do as I have done to you. Very truly, I tell you, servants are not greater than their master, nor are messengers greater than the one who sent them.'

John 13:3–16

🌸 FEBRUARY 15 🌸

'Do not let your hearts be troubled. Believe in God, believe also in me. In my Father's house there are many dwelling places. If it were not so, would I have told you that I go to prepare a place for you?...

'I have said these things to you while I am still with you. But the Advocate, the Holy Spirit, whom the Father will send in my name, will teach you everything, and remind you of all that I have said to you. Peace I leave with you; my peace I give to you. I do not give to you as the world gives. Do not let your hearts be troubled, and do not let them be afraid.'

John 14:1–2, 25–27

🌸 FEBRUARY 16 🌸

'As the Father has loved me, so I have loved you; abide in my love. If you keep my commandments, you will abide in my love, just as I have kept my Father's commandments and abide in his love. I have said these things to you so that my joy may be in you, and that your joy may be complete.

'This is my commandment, that you love one another as I have loved you. No one has greater love than this, to lay down one's life for one's friends. You are my friends if you do what I command you. I do not call you servants any longer, because the servant does not know what the master is doing; but I have called you friends, because I have made known to you everything that I have heard from my Father. You did not choose me but I chose you. And I appointed you to go and bear fruit, fruit that will last, so that the Father will give you whatever you ask him in my name. I am giving you these commands so that you may love one another.'

John 15:9–17

❧ FEBRUARY 17 ❧

Then Jesus went with them to a place called Gethsemane; and he said to his disciples, 'Sit here while I go over there and pray.' He took with him Peter and the two sons of Zebedee, and began to be grieved and agitated. Then he said to them, 'I am deeply grieved, even to death; remain here, and stay awake with me.' And going a little farther, he threw himself on the ground and prayed, 'My Father, if it is possible, let this cup pass from me; yet not what I want but what you want.' Then he came to the disciples and found them sleeping; and he said to Peter, 'So, could you not stay awake with me one hour? Stay awake and pray that you may not come into the time of trial; the spirit indeed is willing, but the flesh is weak.' Again he went away for the second time and prayed, 'My Father, if this cannot pass unless I drink it, your will be done.' Again he came and found them sleeping, for their eyes were heavy. So leaving them again, he went away and prayed for the third time, saying the same words. Then he came to the disciples and said to them, 'Are you still sleeping and taking your rest? See, the hour is at hand, and the Son of Man is betrayed into the hands of sinners. Get up, let us be going. See, my betrayer is at hand.'

Matthew 26:36–46

❧ FEBRUARY 18 ❧

It was very early on the first day of the week and still dark, when Mary of Magdala came to the tomb. She saw that the stone had been moved away from the tomb and came running to Simon Peter and the other disciple, the one whom Jesus loved. 'They have taken the Lord out of the tomb,' she said, 'and we don't know where they have put him.'

So Peter set out with the other disciple to go to the tomb. They ran together, but the other disciple, running faster than Peter, reached the tomb first; he bent down and saw the linen cloths lying on the ground, but did not go in. Simon Peter, following him, also came up, went into the tomb, saw the linen cloths lying on the ground and also the cloth that had been over his head; this was not with the linen cloths but rolled up in a place by itself. Then the other disciple who had reached the tomb first also went in; he saw and he believed. Till this moment they had not understood the scripture, that he must rise from the dead. The disciples then went back home.

But Mary was standing outside near the tomb, weeping. Then, as she wept, she stooped to look inside, and saw two angels in white sitting where the body of Jesus had been, one at the head, the other at the feet. They said, 'Woman, why are you weeping?' 'They have taken my Lord away,' she replied, 'and I don't know where they have put him.' As she said this she turned round and saw Jesus standing there, though she did not realize that it was Jesus. Jesus said to her, 'Woman, why are you weeping? Who are you looking for?' Supposing him to be the gardener, she said, 'Sir, if you have taken him away, tell me where you have put him, and I will go and remove him.' Jesus said, 'Mary!' She turned round then and said to him in Hebrew, 'Rabbuni!' – which means Master. Jesus said to her, 'Do not cling to me, because I have not yet ascended to the Father. But go to the brothers, and tell them: I am ascending to my Father and your Father, to my God and your God.' So Mary of Magdala told the disciples, 'I have seen the Lord,' and that he had said these things to her.

John 20:1–18

❧ FEBRUARY 19 ❧

In the evening of that same day, the first day of the week, the doors were closed in the room where the disciples were, for fear of the Jews. Jesus came and stood among them. He said to them, 'Peace be with you,' and, after saying this, he showed them his hands and his side.

The disciples were filled with joy at seeing the Lord, and he said to them again, 'Peace be with you.

As the Father sent me,
so am I sending you.'

After saying this he breathed on them and said:

Receive the Holy Spirit.
If you forgive anyone's sins,
they are forgiven;
if you retain anyone's sins,
they are retained.

Thomas, called the Twin, who was one of the Twelve, was not with them when Jesus came. So the other disciples said to him, 'We have seen the Lord,' but he answered, 'Unless I can see the holes that the nails made in his hands and can put my finger into the holes they made, and unless I can put my hand into his side, I refuse to believe.' Eight days later the disciples were in the house again and Thomas was with them. The doors were closed, but Jesus came in and stood among them. 'Peace be with you,' he said. Then he spoke to Thomas, 'Put your finger here; look, here are my hands. Give me your hand; put it into my side. Do not be unbelieving any more but believe.' Thomas replied, 'My Lord and my God!' Jesus said to him:

You believe because you can see me.
Blessed are those who have not seen me
    and yet believe.

John 20:19–29

❦ FEBRUARY 20 ❦

Now on that same day two of them were going to a village called Emmaus, about seven miles from Jerusalem, and talking with each other about all these things that had happened. While they were talking and discussing, Jesus himself came near and went with them, but their eyes were kept from recognizing him. And he said to them, 'What are you discussing with each other while you walk along?' They stood still, looking sad. Then one of them, whose name was Cleopas, answered him, 'Are you the only stranger in Jerusalem who does not know the things that have taken place there in these days?' He asked them, 'What things?' They replied, 'The things about Jesus of Nazareth, who was a prophet mighty in deed and word before God and all the people, and how our chief priests and leaders handed him over to be condemned to death and crucified him. But we had hoped that he was the one to redeem Israel. Yes, and besides all this, it is now the third day since these things took place. Moreover, some women of our group astounded us. They were at the tomb early this morning, and when they did not find his body there, they came back and told us that they had indeed seen a vision of angels who said that he was alive. Some of those who were with us went to the tomb and found it just as the women had said; but they did not see him.' Then he said to them, 'Oh, how foolish you are, and how slow of heart to believe all that the prophets have declared! Was it not necessary that the Messiah should suffer these things and then enter into his glory?' Then beginning with Moses and all the prophets, he interpreted to them the things about himself in all the scriptures.

As they came near the village to which they were going, he walked ahead as if he were going on. But they urged him strongly, saying, 'Stay with us, because it is almost evening and the day is now nearly over.' So he went in to stay with them. When he was at the table with them, he took bread, blessed and broke it, and gave it to them. Then their eyes were opened, and they recognized him; and he vanished from their sight. They said to each other, 'Were not our hearts burning within us while he was talking to us on the road, while he was opening the scriptures to us?'

Luke 24:13–32

❧ FEBRUARY 21 ❧

I consider that the sufferings of this present time are not worth comparing with the glory about to be revealed to us. For the creation waits with eager longing for the revealing of the children of God; for the creation was subjected to futility, not of its own will but by the will of the one who subjected it, in hope that the creation itself will be set free from its bondage to decay and will obtain the freedom of the glory of the children of God. We know that the whole creation has been groaning in labour pains until now; and not only the creation, but we ourselves, who have the first fruits of the Spirit, groan inwardly while we wait for adoption, the redemption of our bodies. For in hope we were saved. Now hope that is seen is not hope. For who hopes for what is seen? But if we hope for what we do not see, we wait for it with patience.

Romans 8:18–25

FEBRUARY 22

Finally, be strong in the Lord and in the strength of his power. Put on the whole armour of God, so that you may be able to stand against the wiles of the devil. For our struggle is not against enemies of blood and flesh, but against the rulers, against the authorities, against the cosmic powers of this present darkness, against the spiritual forces of evil in the heavenly places. Therefore take up the whole armour of God, so that you may be able to withstand on that evil day, and having done everything, to stand firm. Stand therefore, and fasten the belt of truth around your waist, and put on the breastplate of righteousness. As shoes for your feet put on whatever will make you ready to proclaim the gospel of peace. With all of these, take the shield of faith, with which you will be able to quench all the flaming arrows of the evil one. Take the helmet of salvation, and the sword of the Spirit, which is the word of God.

Pray in the Spirit at all times in every prayer and supplication. To that end keep alert and always persevere in supplication for all the saints.

Ephesians 6:10–18

FEBRUARY 23

For the message about the cross is foolishness to those who are perishing, but to us who are being saved it is the power of God. For it is written,

'I will destroy the wisdom of the wise,
    and the discernment of the
    discerning I will thwart.'

Where is the one who is wise? Where is the scribe? Where is the debater of this age? Has not God made foolish the wisdom of the world? For since, in the wisdom of God, the world did not know God through wisdom, God decided, through the foolishness of our proclamation, to save those who believe. For Jews demand signs and Greeks desire wisdom, but we proclaim Christ crucified, a stumbling-block to Jews and foolishness to Gentiles, but to those who are the called, both Jews and Greeks, Christ the power of God and the wisdom of God. For God's foolishness is wiser than human wisdom, and God's weakness is stronger than human strength.

Consider your own call, brothers and sisters: not many of you were wise by human standards, not many were powerful, not many were of noble birth. But God chose what is foolish in the world to shame the wise; God chose what is weak in the world to shame the strong…

1 Corinthians 1:18–27

❧   FEBRUARY 24   ❧

Now there are varieties of gifts, but the same Spirit; and there are varieties of services, but the same Lord; and there are varieties of activities, but it is the same God who activates all of them in everyone. To each is given the manifestation of the Spirit for the common good. To one is given through the Spirit the utterance of wisdom, and to another the utterance of knowledge according to the same Spirit, to another faith by the same Spirit, to another gifts of healing by the one Spirit, to another the working of miracles, to another prophecy, to another the discernment of spirits, to another various kinds of tongues, to another the interpretation of tongues. All these are activated by one and the same Spirit, who allots to each one individually just as the Spirit chooses.

1 Corinthians 12:4–11

FEBRUARY 25

If I speak in the tongues of mortals and of angels, but do not have love, I am a noisy gong or a clanging cymbal. And if I have prophetic powers, and understand all mysteries and all knowledge, and if I have all faith, so as to remove mountains, but do not have love, I am nothing. If I give away all my possessions, and if I hand over my body so that I may boast, but do not have love, I gain nothing.

Love is patient; love is kind; love is not envious or boastful or arrogant or rude. It does not insist on its own way; it is not irritable or resentful; it does not rejoice in wrongdoing, but rejoices in the truth. It bears all things, believes all things, hopes all things, endures all things.

Love never ends. But as for prophecies, they will come to an end; as for tongues, they will cease; as for knowledge, it will come to an end. For we know only in part, and we prophesy only in part; but when the complete comes, the partial will come to an end. When I was a child, I spoke like a child, I thought like a child, I reasoned like a child; when I became an adult, I put an end to childish ways. For now we see in a mirror, dimly, but then we will see face to face. Now I know only in part; then I will know fully, even as I have been fully known. And now faith, hope, and love abide, these three; and the greatest of these is love.

1 Corinthians 13

FEBRUARY 26

If then there is any encouragement in Christ, any consolation from love, any sharing in the Spirit, any compassion and sympathy, make my joy complete: be of the same mind, having the same love, being in full accord and of one mind. Do nothing from selfish ambition or conceit, but in humility regard others as better than yourselves. Let each of you look not to your own interests, but to the interests of others. Let the same mind be in you that was in Christ Jesus,

who, though he was in the form of God,
did not regard equality with God
as something to be exploited,

but emptied himself,
    taking the form of a slave,
    being born in human likeness.
And being found in human form,
    he humbled himself
    and became obedient to the point of death –
    even death on a cross.

Therefore God also highly exalted him
    and gave him the name
    that is above every name,
so that at the name of Jesus
    every knee should bend,
    in heaven and on earth and under the earth,
and every tongue should confess
    that Jesus Christ is Lord,
    to the glory of God the Father.

Philippians 2:1–11

🌸 FEBRUARY 27 🌸

Now faith is the assurance of things hoped for, the conviction of things not seen. Indeed, by faith our ancestors received approval. By faith we understand that the worlds were prepared by the word of God, so that what is seen was made from things that are not visible...

By faith Abraham obeyed when he was called to set out for a place that he was to receive as an inheritance; and he set out, not knowing where he was going. By faith he stayed for a time in the land he had been promised, as in a foreign land, living in tents, as did Isaac and Jacob, who were heirs with him of the same promise. For he looked forward to the city that has foundations, whose architect and builder is God. By faith he received power of procreation, even though he was too old – and Sarah herself was barren – because he considered him faithful who had promised. Therefore from one person, and this one as good as dead, descendants were born, 'as many as the stars of heaven and as the innumerable grains of sand by the seashore.'

All of these died in faith without having received the promises, but from a distance they saw and greeted them. They confessed that they were strangers and foreigners on the earth, for people who speak in this way make it clear that they are seeking a homeland.

Hebrews 11:1–3, 8–14

FEBRUARY 28

Then I saw a new heaven and a new earth; for the first heaven and the first earth had passed away, and the sea was no more. And I saw the holy city, the new Jerusalem, coming down out of heaven from God, prepared as a bride adorned for her husband. And I heard a loud voice from the throne saying,

'See, the home of God is among mortals.
He will dwell with them;
they will be his peoples,
and God himself will be with them;
he will wipe every tear from their eyes.
Death will be no more;
mourning and crying and pain will be no more,
for the first things have passed away.'

And the one who was seated on the throne said, 'See, I am making all things new.' Also he said, 'Write this, for these words are trustworthy and true.' Then he said to me, 'It is done! I am the Alpha and the Omega, the beginning and the end. To the thirsty I will give water as a gift from the spring of the water of life. Those who conquer will inherit these things, and I will be their God and they will be my children.'

Revelation 21:1–7

MARCH

Reflections from the Desert Fathers and Mothers

MARCH 1

Antony was left alone, after his parents' death, with one quite young sister. He was about eighteen or even twenty years old, and he was responsible both for the home and his sister. Six months had not passed since the death of his parents when, going to the Lord's house as usual and gathering his thoughts, he considered while he walked how the apostles, forsaking everything, followed the Saviour, and how in Acts some sold what they possessed and took the proceeds and placed them at the feet of the apostles for distribution among those in need, and what great hope is stored up for such people in heaven. He went into the church pondering these things, and just then it happened that the Gospel was being read, and he heard the Lord saying to the rich man, 'If you would be perfect, go, sell what you possess and give to the poor, and you will have treasure in heaven.' It was as if by God's design he held the saints in his recollection, and as if the passage were read on his account. Immediately Antony went out from the Lord's house and gave to the townspeople the possessions he had from his forbears (three hundred fertile and very beautiful [arourae]), so that they would not disturb him or his sister in the least. And selling all the rest that was portable, when he had collected sufficient money, he donated it to the poor, keeping a few things for his sister.

Athanasius (296–373), Life of Antony

MARCH 2

There were not yet many monasteries in Egypt, and no monk knew at all the great desert, but each of those wishing to give attention to his life disciplined himself in isolation, not far from his own village. Now at that time in the neighbouring village there was an old man who had practised from his youth the solitary life. When Antony saw him, he emulated him in goodness. At first he also began by remaining in places proximate to his village. And going forth from there, if he heard of some zealous person anywhere, he searched him out like the wise bee. He did not go back to his own place unless he had seen him, and as though receiving from him certain supplies for travelling the road to virtue, he returned. He weighed in his thoughts how he would not look back on things of his parents, nor call his relatives to memory. He worked with his hands, though, having heard that he who is idle, let him not eat. And he spent what he made partly for bread, and partly on those in need. He prayed constantly, since he learned that it is necessary to pray unceasingly in private.

Athanasius (296–373), Life of Antony

🎕 MARCH 3 🎕

The devil, who despises and envies good, could not bear seeing such purpose in a youth, but the sort of things he had busied himself in doing in the past, he set to work to do against this person as well. First he attempted to lead him away from the discipline, suggesting memories of his possessions, the guardianship of his sister, the bonds of kinship, love of money and of glory, the manifold pleasure of food, the relaxations of life, and, finally, the rigour of virtue, and how great the labour is that earns it, suggesting also the bodily weakness and the length of time involved. Then he placed his confidence in the weapons in the navel of his belly. The one hurled foul thoughts and the other overturned them through his prayers; the former resorted to titillation, but the latter, seeming to blush, fortified the body with faith and with prayers and fasting… in thinking about the Christ and considering the excellence won through him, and the intellectual part of the soul, Antony extinguished the fire of his opponent's deception.

Athanasius (296–373), Life of Antony

🎕 MARCH 4 🎕

[Antony] hurried towards the mountain. When he discovered beyond the river a deserted fortress, empty so long that reptiles filled it, he went there, and took up residence in it. Then at once the creeping things departed, as if someone were in pursuit, and barricading the entrance once more, and putting aside enough loaves for six months (for the Thebans do this, and frequently they remain unspoiled for a whole year), and having water inside, he was hidden within as in a shrine. He remained alone in the place, neither going out himself nor seeing any of those who visited. For a long time he continued this life of discipline, receiving the loaves twice yearly from the housetop above. Nearly twenty years he spent in this manner... After this... Antony came forth as though from a shrine, having been led into divine mysteries and inspired by God.

Athanasius (296–373), Life of Antony

❦ MARCH 5 ❦

One day when [Antony] had gone out, all the monks came to him, asking to hear a discourse. In the Egyptian tongue he told them these things. 'The scriptures are sufficient for instruction, but it is good for us to encourage each other in the faith. Now you, saying what you know, bring this to the father like children, and I, as your elder, will share what I know and the fruits of my experience. In the first place, let us hold in common the same eagerness not to surrender what we have begun, either by growing fainthearted in the labours or by saying, "We have spent a long time in the discipline." Rather, as though making a beginning daily, let us increase our dedication. For the entire life span of men is very brief when measured against the ages to come, so that all our time is nothing in comparison with eternal life.'

Athanasius (296–373), Life of Antony

❦ MARCH 6 ❦

All rejoiced while Antony talked about these things. In some, the love of virtue increased, in others carelessness was discarded, and in still others conceit was brought to an end. And all were persuaded to hate the demonic conniving, marvelling at the grace given by the Lord to

Antony for the discernment of spirits. So their cells in the hills were like tents filled with divine choirs – people chanting, studying, fasting, praying, rejoicing in the hope of future boons, working for the distribution of alms, and maintaining both love and harmony among themselves. It was as if one truly looked on a land all its own, a land of devotion and righteousness. For neither perpetrator nor victim of injustice was there, nor complaint of a tax collector. And there was a multitude of ascetics, but among them all there was one mind, and it was set on virtue.

Athanasius (296–373), Life of Antony

🏵 MARCH 7 🏵

A brother asked one of the elders: 'What good thing shall I do, and have life thereby?' The old man replied: 'God alone knows what is good. However, I have heard it said that someone inquired of Father Abba Nisteros the great, the friend of Abba Anthony, asking: "What good work shall I do?" and that he replied: "Not all works are alike. For scripture says that Abraham was hospitable and God was with him. Elias loved solitary prayer, and God was with him. And David was humble, and God was with him. Therefore, whatever you see your soul to desire according to God, do that thing, and you shall keep your heart safe."'

The Wisdom of the Desert

🏵 MARCH 8 🏵

A certain brother came to Abba Silvanus at Mount Sinai, and seeing the hermits at work he exclaimed: 'Why do you work for the bread that perisheth? "Mary has chosen the best part, namely to sit at the feet of the Lord without working."' Then the abba said to his disciple Zachary: 'Give the brother a book and let him read, and put him in an empty cell.' At the ninth hour the brother who was reading began to look out to see if the abba was not going to call him to dinner, and sometime

after the ninth hour he went to the abba and said: 'Did the brethren not eat today, Father?' 'Oh yes, certainly,' said the abba, 'they just had dinner.' 'Well,' said the brother, 'why did you not call me?' 'You are a spiritual man,' said the abba, 'you don't need this food that perisheth. We have to work, but you have chosen the better part. You read all day, and can get along without food.' Hearing this the brother said: 'Forgive me, Father.' And the abba said: 'Martha is necessary to Mary, for it was because Martha worked that Mary was able to be praised.'
[See February 13]

The Wisdom of the Desert

❧ MARCH 9 ❧

A brother came to Abba Pastor and said: 'Many distracting thoughts come into my mind, and I am in danger because of them.' Then the elder thrust him out into the open air and said: 'Open up the garments about your chest and catch the wind in them.' But he replied: 'This I cannot do.' So the elder said to him:' If you cannot catch the wind, neither can you prevent distracting thoughts from coming into your head. Your job is to say No to them.'

The Wisdom of the Desert

❧ MARCH 10 ❧

Abbess Syncletica of holy memory said: 'There is labour and great struggle for the impious who are converted to God, but after that comes inexpressible joy. A man who wants to light a fire first is plagued by smoke, and the smoke drives him to tears, yet finally he gets the fire that he wants. So also it is written: "Our God is a consuming fire." Hence we ought to light the divine fire in ourselves with labour and with tears.'

The Wisdom of the Desert

❧ MARCH 11 ❧

Abba Pastor said that Abba John the Dwarf had prayed to the Lord and the Lord had taken away all his passions, so that he became impassible. And in this condition he went to one of the elders and said: 'You see before you a man who is completely at rest and has no more temptations.' The elder said: 'Go and pray to the Lord to command some struggle to be stirred up in you, for the soul is matured only in battles.' And when the temptations started up again he did not pray that the struggle be taken away from him, but only said: 'Lord, give me strength to get through the fight.'

The Wisdom of the Desert

❧ MARCH 12 ❧

Once Abba Anthony was conversing with some brethren, and a hunter who was after game in the wilderness came upon them. He saw Abba Anthony and the brothers enjoying themselves, and disapproved. Abba Anthony said: 'Put an arrow in your bow and shoot it.' This he did. 'Now shoot another,' said the elder. 'And another, and another.' The hunter said: 'If I bend my bow all the time it will break.' Abba Anthony replied: 'So it is in the work of God. If we push ourselves beyond measure, the brethren will soon collapse. It is right, therefore, from time to time, to relax their efforts.'

The Wisdom of the Desert

❧ MARCH 13 ❧

One of the fathers related this: 'Once when I was at Oxyrhyncus, some poor people came on Saturday evening to receive charity. We were lying down, and there was one of them who only had a single mat, half underneath and half on top of him. Now it was cold, and when I went out for my natural needs, I heard his teeth chattering because of the severe cold, and he was encouraging himself, saying, "I thank you, Lord: how many rich people are in prison wearing irons at present; how many more have their feet fastened to wood, not being able so much as to satisfy their bodily needs whereas I am like a king with my legs stretched out." When I heard this, I recounted it to the brethren and they were edified.'

The Wisdom of the Desert Fathers

🞴 MARCH 14 🞴

A brother asked one of the Fathers if one is defiled by having evil thoughts. There was a discussion on the subject, and someone said, 'Yes, one is defiled', and others, 'No, or else poor men that we are we could not be saved; what counts is not to carry them out corporally.' The brother went to a very experienced old man to question him about the discussion. The old man said to him, 'What is required of each one is regulated according to his capacity.' The brother begged the old man to explain saying, 'For the Lord's sake, explain this saying.' The old man said to him, 'Suppose a tempting object is placed here and two brothers, of whom one is more advanced in virtue than the other, come in. He who is perfect says to himself, 'I should very much like to have this object', but he does not rest in this thought; he cuts it off at once and he is not defiled; but if he who has not yet come to this measure desires the object and his thought clings to it still if he does not take it he also is not defiled.'

The Wisdom of the Desert Fathers

🞴 MARCH 15 🞴

Someone asked Abba Anthony, 'What must one do in order to please God?' The old man replied, 'Pay attention to what I tell you: whoever you may be, always have God before your eyes; whatever you do, do it according to the testimony of the holy scriptures; in whatever place you live, do not easily leave it. Keep these three precepts and you will be saved.'

The Sayings of the Desert Fathers, Abba Anthony

❀ MARCH 16 ❀

One day some old men came to see Abba Anthony. In the midst of them was Abba Joseph. Wanting to test them, the old man suggested a text from the scriptures and, beginning with the youngest, he asked them what it meant.

Each gave his opinion as he was able. But to each one the old man said, 'You have not understood it.' Last of all he said to Abba Joseph, 'How would you explain this saying?' and he replied, 'I do not know.' Then Abba Anthony said, 'Indeed, Abba Joseph has found the way, for he said: "I do not know."'

The Sayings of the Desert Fathers, Abba Anthony

❀ MARCH 17 ❀

Three old men, of whom one had a bad reputation, came one day to Abba Achilles. The first asked him, 'Father, make me a fishing-net.' 'I will not make you one,' he replied. Then the second said, 'Of your charity make one, so that we may have a souvenir of you in the monastery.' But he said, 'I do not have time.' Then the third one, who had a bad reputation, said, 'Make me a fishing-net, so that I may have something from your hands, Father.' Abba Achilles answered him at once, 'For you I will make one.' Then the two other old men asked him privately, 'Why did you not want to do what we asked you, but you promised to do what he asked?'

The old man gave them this answer, 'I told you I would not make one, and you were not disappointed, since you thought that I had no time. But if I had not made one for him, he would have said, "The old man has heard about my sin, and that is why he does not want to make me anything," and so our relationship would have broken down. But now I have cheered his soul, so that he will not be overcome with grief.'

The Sayings of the Desert Fathers, Abba Achilles

MARCH 18

Abba Zeno said, 'If a man wants God to hear his prayer quickly, then before he prays for anything else, even his own soul, when he stands and stretches out his hands towards God, he must pray with all his heart for his enemies. Through this action God will hear everything that he asks.'

The Sayings of the Desert Fathers, Abba Zeno

MARCH 19

A brother lived in the Cells and in his solitude he was troubled. He went to tell Abba Theodore of Pherme about it. The old man said to him, 'Go, be more humble in your aspirations, place yourself under obedience and live with others.' Later, he came back to the old man and said, 'I do not find any peace with others.' The old man said to him, 'If you are not at peace either alone or with others, why have you become a monk? Is it not to suffer trials? Tell me how many years you have worn the habit?' He replied, 'For eight years.' Then the old man said to him, 'I have worn the habit seventy years and on no day have I found peace. Do you expect to obtain peace in eight years?' At these words the brother went away strengthened.

The Sayings of the Desert Fathers, Abba Theodore

MARCH 20

Abba Theophilus, the archbishop, came to Scetis one day. The brethren who were assembled said to Abba Pambo, 'Say something to the archbishop, so that he may be edified.' The old man said to them, 'If he is not edified by my silence, he will not be edified by my speech.'

The Sayings of the Desert Fathers, Abba Theophilus

MARCH 21

Abba John the Dwarf said, 'A house is not built by beginning at the top and working down. You must begin with the foundations in order to reach the top.' They said to him, 'What does this saying mean?' He said, 'The foundation is our neighbour, whom we must win, and that is the place to begin. For all the commandments of Christ depend on this one.'

The Sayings of the Desert Fathers, Abba John the Dwarf

MARCH 22

The old man said that there were three philosophers who were friends. The first died and left his son to the care of one of the others. When he grew up he had intercourse with the wife of his guardian, who found them out and turned the boy out of doors. Although the young man came and asked his guardian to forgive him he would not receive him, but said, 'Go and work for three years as a ferryman and I will forgive you.'

After three years the young man came to him again, and this time he said, 'You still have not done enough penance; go and work for three years, and give away all you earn, bearing all insults.' So he did this, and then his guardian said to him, 'Now go to Athens and learn philosophy.'

There was an old man who sat at the philosophers' gate and he used to insult everyone who entered it. When he insulted this young man, the boy began to laugh, and the old man said, 'Why are you laughing, when I have insulted you?' He told him, 'Would you not expect me to laugh? For three years I have paid to be insulted and now I am insulted free of charge. That is why I laughed.'

Abba John said, 'The gate of the Lord is like that, and we Fathers go through many insults in order to enter joyfully into the city of God.'

The Sayings of the Desert Fathers, Abba John the Dwarf

MARCH 23

Abba Lot went to see Abba Joseph and said to him, 'Abba, as far as I can I say my little office, I fast a little, I pray and meditate, I live in peace and as far as I can, I purify my thoughts. What else can I do?' Then the old man stood up and stretched his hands towards heaven. His fingers became like ten lamps of fire and he said to him, 'If you will, you can become all flame.'

The Sayings of the Desert Fathers, Abba Joseph of Panephysis

MARCH 24

Abba Joseph the Theban said, 'Three works are approved in the eyes of the Lord; when a man is ill and temptations fall upon him, if he welcomes them with gratitude; secondly, when someone carries out all his works purely in the presence of God, having no regard for anything human; in the third place, when someone remains in submission to a spiritual father in complete renunciation of his own will. This last will gain a lofty crown indeed. As for me, I have chosen illness.'

The Sayings of the Desert Fathers, Abba Joseph the Theban

MARCH 25

Abba Macarius was asked, 'How should one pray?' The old man said, 'There is no need at all to make long discourses; it is enough to stretch out one's hands and say, "Lord, as you will, and as you know, have mercy." And if the conflict grows fiercer say "Lord, help!" He knows very well what we need and he shews us his mercy.'

The Sayings of the Desert Fathers, Abba Macarius

❦ MARCH 26 ❧

A brother at Scetis committed a fault. A council was called to which Abba Moses was invited, but he refused to go to it. Then the priest sent someone to say to him, 'Come, for everyone is waiting for you.' So he got up and went. He took a leaking jug, filled it with water and carried it with him. The others came out to meet him and said to him, 'What is this, Father?' The old man said to them, 'My sins run out behind me, and I do not see them, and today I am coming to judge the errors of another.' When they heard that they said no more to the brother but forgave him.

The Sayings of the Desert Fathers, Abba Moses

❦ MARCH 27 ❧

A brother came to Scetis to visit Abba Moses and asked him for a word. The old man said to him, 'Go, sit in your cell, and your cell will teach you everything.'

The Sayings of the Desert Fathers, Abba Moses

❦ MARCH 28 ❧

He also said that Abba Isidore, the priest of Scetis, spoke to the people one day saying, 'Brothers, is it not in order to endure affliction that we have come to this place? But now there is no affliction for us here. So I am getting my sheepskin ready to go where there is some affliction and there I shall find peace.'

The Sayings of the Desert Fathers, Abba Poemen

✦ MARCH 29 ✦

He said that someone asked Abba Paesius, 'What should I do about my soul, because it is insensitive and does not fear God?' He said to him, 'Go, and join a man who fears God, and live near him; he will teach you, too, to fear God.'

The Sayings of the Desert Fathers, Abba Poemen

✦ MARCH 30 ✦

A brother questioned Abba Poemen saying, 'What does it mean to be angry with your brother without a cause?' He said, 'If your brother hurts you by his arrogance and you are angry with him because of it, that is getting angry without cause. If he plucks out your right eye and cuts off your right hand, and you get angry with him, you are angry without cause. But if he separates you from God, then be angry with him.'

The Sayings of the Desert Fathers, Abba Poemen

✦ MARCH 31 ✦

One of the fathers asked Abba Sisoes, 'If I am sitting in the desert and a barbarian comes to kill me and if I am stronger than he, shall I kill him?' The old man said to him, 'No, leave him to God. In fact whatever the trial is which comes to a man, let him say, "This has happened to me because of my sins," and if something good comes say, "It is through the providence of God."'

The Sayings of the Desert Fathers, Abba Sisoes

APRIL

Reflections from Medieval Saints

✿ APRIL 1 ✿

Martin was an officer in the Roman army. One day he was riding with his regiment, in bitterly cold weather, when they came across a naked beggar, by the road-side, freezing to death. Moved with pity, Martin got off his horse, and went up to him. He cut his warm cloak in half with his sword, and wrapped the beggar up in it. Then he hurried back to join his men.

That night Martin had a dream. He dreamed that he saw Christ talking with the angels, and Christ was wearing the half a cloak that Martin had given to the beggar! Martin overheard Christ explain to the angels that he had been bitterly cold, almost to the point of death, but that Martin had come along and saved his life by giving him half his cloak. 'And the amazing thing is,' Christ concluded, 'that Martin isn't even a follower of mine yet.'

When Martin awoke in the morning, he resolved to be baptized.

Author's retelling

✿ APRIL 2 ✿

I [Patrick] was taken into captivity to Ireland with many thousands of people. We deserved this fate because we had turned away from God; we neither kept his commandments nor obeyed our pastors who used to warn us about our salvation. The Lord's fury boiled over on us and he scattered us among many nations, even to the ends of the earth. This is where I now am, in all my insignificance, among strangers. The Lord there made me aware of my unbelief that I might at last advert to my sins and turn wholeheartedly to the Lord my God. He showed concern for my weakness, and pity for my youth and ignorance; he watched over me before I got to know him…

When I had come to Ireland I tended herds every day and I used to pray many times during the day. More and more my love of God and reverence for him began to increase. My faith grew stronger and my zeal so intense that in the course of a single day I would say as many as a hundred prayers, and almost as many in the night. This I did even when I was in the woods and on the mountains. Even in times of snow or frost or rain I would rise before dawn to pray. I never felt the worse for it; nor was I in any way lazy because, as I now realize, I was full of enthusiasm.

Patrick (390–460)

APRIL 3

From his boyhood Colum Cille devoted himself to the Christian combat and to the search for wisdom. By God's grace he preserved integrity of body and purity of soul, so that he seemed like one ready for the life of heaven though still on earth; for in appearance he was like an angel, refined in his speech, holy in his works, pre-eminent in character, great in counsel.

In the forty-second year of his age he sailed away from Ireland to Britain, wishing to be a pilgrim for Christ. During his life of thirty-four years as a soldier of Christ on the island of Iona, he could not let even one hour pass that was not given to prayer or reading or writing or some other good work. Night and day he so unwearyingly gave himself to fasts and vigils that the burden of each single work seemed beyond the strength of man. Yet through all he was loving to everyone, his holy face was always cheerful. And in his inmost heart he was happy with joy of the Holy Spirit.

Adamnan (625–704), The Life of Columba

APRIL 4

The life in David's monastery was noted for its severity, nevertheless many came to join the community. Rhigyfarch, in his *Life of St David* [c. 1290], gives us an account of the life of the monks. They tilled the land all day, using no oxen, but yoking themselves to the plough. They worked in silence, and none possessed any property of his own. When the work outside was done they went in and occupied themselves with reading and writing until evening. Then they went to their devotions in church, remaining there 'until the stars are seen in heaven bringing the day to a close.' Their supper was bread and herbs and water, and after it they spent three hours in church. Then they slept until cockcrow.

David himself led a more austere life than any, following the way of life of the Egyptian desert communities. He spent much time in prayer and in teaching his monks, and he cared for and taught and fed all the needy folk and pilgrims who came to his monastery.

A Book of Welsh Saints

APRIL 5

As soon as [Augustine and his companions] had occupied the house given to them they began to emulate the life of the apostles and the primitive Church. They were constantly at prayer; they fasted and kept vigils; they preached the word of life to whomsoever they could. They regarded worldly things as of little importance, and accepted only the necessities of life from those they taught. They practised what they preached, and were willing to endure any hardship, and even to die for the truth which they proclaimed. Before long a number of heathen, admiring the simplicity of their lives and the comfort of their heavenly message, believed and were baptized. On the east side of the city stood an old church, built in honour of Saint Martin during the Roman occupation of Britain, where the Christian Queen went to pray. Here they first assembled to sing the psalms, to pray, to say Mass, to preach, and to baptize, until the king's own conversion to the Faith gave them greater freedom to preach and to build and restore churches everywhere.

Bede (673–735), A History of the English Church and People

APRIL 6

Bishop Aidan gave his clergy an inspiring example of self-discipline and continence, and the highest recommendation of his teaching to all was that he and his followers lived as they taught. He never sought or cared for any worldly possessions, and loved to give away to the poor who chanced to meet him whatever he received from kings or wealthy folk. Whether in town or country, he always travelled on foot unless compelled by necessity to ride; and whatever people he met on his walks, whether high or low, he stopped and spoke to them. If they were heathen, he urged them to be baptized; and if they were Christians, he strengthened their faith, and inspired them by word and deed to live a good life and to be generous to others.

Bede (673–735), A History of the English Church and People

🌿 APRIL 7 🌿

In addition to Chad's many virtues, of continence, humility, right preaching, prayer, voluntary poverty, and many others, he was so filled with the fear of God and so mindful of his last end in all that he did, that I was told by one of his monks named Trumbert – who was one of my tutors in the scriptures and had been trained in the monastery under Chad's direction – that, if a gale arose while he was reading or doing anything else, he would at once call upon God for mercy and pray him to show mercy on mankind. And if the wind increased in violence, he would close his book and prostrate himself on the ground, praying even more earnestly. But if there was a violent storm of wind and rain, or thunder and lightning startled earth and air, he would go to the church and devote all his thoughts to prayers and psalms continuously until the tempest had passed.

Bede (673–735), A History of the English Church and People

🌿 APRIL 8 🌿

Once the brethren had helped [Cuthbert] to build the place, he lived completely alone. At first, if they came over to visit him, he would go out and see to their needs; he would, for instance, wash their feet in warm water. Sometimes they made him take off his shoes and let them return the compliment, for care of his own body was so far from his thoughts that he kept his soft leather boots on his feet for months on end without ever removing them. If he put new boots on at Easter they would not come off till the next Easter and then only for the Washing of the Feet in church on Maundy Thursday. The monks found long calluses, where the boots had chafed his shins through all his prayers and genuflections.

Bede (673–735), The Life of Cuthbert

❧ APRIL 9 ❧

'Your Majesty, when we compare the present life of man on earth with that time of which we have no knowledge, it seems to me like the swift flight of a single sparrow through the banqueting-hall where you are sitting at dinner on a winter's day with your thanes and counsellors. In the midst there is a comforting fire to warm the hall; outside, the storms of winter rain or snow are raging. This sparrow flies swiftly in through one door of the hall, and out through another. While he is inside, he is safe from the winter storms; but after a few moments of comfort, he vanishes from sight into the wintry world from which he came. Even so, man appears on earth for a little while; but of what went before this life or of what follows, we know nothing. Therefore, if this new teaching has brought any more certain knowledge, it seems only right that we should follow it.'

Bede (673–735), A History of the English Church and People

❧ APRIL 10 ❧

Christ's servant Abbess Hilda, whom all her acquaintances called Mother because of her wonderful devotion and grace, was not only an example of holy life to members of her own community; for she also brought about the amendment and salvation of many living at a distance, who heard the inspiring story of her industry and goodness...

When Hilda had ruled this monastery for many years, it pleased the Author of our salvation to try her soul by a long sickness, in order that, as with the Apostle, her strength might be made perfect in weakness. She was attacked by a burning fever that racked her continually for six years; but during all this time she never ceased to give thanks to her Maker or to instruct the flock committed to her, both privately and publicly. For her own example taught them all to serve God obediently when in health, and to render thanks to him faithfully when in trouble or bodily weakness. In the seventh year of her illness the pain passed into her innermost parts, and her last day came. About cockcrow she received the Viaticum of the Holy Communion, and when she had summoned all the handmaids of Christ in the monastery, she urged them to maintain the gospel peace among themselves and with others. And while she was still speaking, she joyfully welcomed death, or rather, in the words of our Lord, passed from death to life.

Bede (673–735), *A History of the English Church and People*

🏵 APRIL 11 🏵

By what signs, under what forms, shall I seek you?
I have never seen you, O Lord my God,
I have never seen your face.
Most High Lord,
what shall an exile do
who is as far away from you as this?
What shall your servant do,
eager for your love, cast off far from your face?
He longs to see you,
but your countenance is too far away.
He wants to have access to you,
but your dwelling is inaccessible.
He longs to find you,
but he does not know where you are.
He loves to seek you,
but he does not know your face.
Lord, you are my Lord and my God,
and I have never seen you.

You have created and re-created me,
all the good I have comes from you,
and still I do not know you.
I was created to see you,
and I have not yet accomplished that for which I was made.

Anselm (1033–1109), Proslogion

❧ APRIL 12 ❧

Let me discern your light,
whether from afar or from the depths.
Teach me to seek you,
and as I seek you, show yourself to me,
for I cannot seek you unless you show me how,
and I will never find you
unless you show yourself to me.
Let me seek you by desiring you,
and desire you by seeking you;
let me find you by loving you,
and love you in finding you.

Anselm (1033–1109), Proslogion

❧ APRIL 13 ❧

'Come to him and you will be illumined, and your faces will not be confounded.' I am, I am confounded, Lord, I am thrown into a black pit of confusion as often as I turn to you and find the door of vision closed to me; it is almost as though I heard those fearful words: 'Truly, I say to you, I know you not.' And because of my longing illumined by you, my heart's hurt and my mental disarray are such as to plunge me into total darkness, where it almost seems that it would have been better for me if I had not come at all. For who is there to console me if you would have me desolate? I will have no solace, none, that is not you yourself or sent from you. Let them all perish in the earth! 'Woe to him who is alone', says Solomon. And woe to me who am indeed alone if you are not with me or I with you. Twice and thrice blessed do I hold myself, O Lord, if I feel you with me, but self-disgust and loathing fill my soul whenever I feel that I am not with you. As long as I am with you, I am present to myself; I am not wholly me when I am not with you. Woe to me each and every time that I am not with you, without whom I cannot even be. I should not be able to subsist in any way at all, either in body or in soul, without the indwelling of your power. Were it not for the presence of your grace in me I should neither desire nor seek you; nor should I ever find you unless your mercy and goodness came to me. But when in these ways I am with you, I feel your grace at work within me, and then I am glad I am, and am alive; my soul gives praise to the Lord. If, however, you are present to me, working for my good, and I am absent, either in thought or feeling, then the very benefits with which your grace surrounds me seem to me like burial rites punctiliously performed over a corpse.

William of St Thierry (1085–1148), Three Meditations

🌼 APRIL 14 🌺

And if from time to time I sense you [God] passing by, you do not pause for me but carry on your way, leaving me like the Canaanite woman crying in your wake. And when I have importuned you to weariness with shouting out my needs, you reproach the sullied conscience of the creature that I am with past depravity and present impudence and drive your dog from the table – or let it take itself off – unfed and famished and stung by conscience' lash. Should I, in that case, come back again? Yes, surely, Lord. For even the whelps whipped from their master's house return at once and, keeping watchful guard over the place, receive their daily bread. So I, thrown out, come back; shut out, I yelp, and whipped off, fawn. A dog cannot live without man's companionship, and nor can my soul without the Lord its God. Open to me therefore, Lord, that I may come to you and be illumined by you.

William of St Thierry (1085–1148), Three Meditations

In consequence there can be no true happiness for the man without a friend. Those who have none to share in their good fortune or their grief, none on to whom they can unload their troubles, no one to whom they can communicate some sudden glorious illumination are like brute beasts. Woe unto him who is alone, for when he falls he has none to lift him up! The man without a friend is a man utterly alone. But what happiness, security and joy to have another self to talk with! One to whom you can confess a failure without fear and reveal unblushingly some progress that you may have made in the spiritual life; someone to whom you dare entrust all the secrets of your heart and in whose advice you can have confidence. But better still by far is the fact that friendship is at one remove from the perfection that is rooted in the knowledge and love of God; for our Saviour says in the Gospel, 'I do not call you servants, but friends', showing that human friendship leads to that of God.

Aelred of Rievaulx (1109–1167), On Spiritual Friendship

Those who are worthy of friendship are loved for qualities inherent in them. Nevertheless, it does quite often happen that vices surface in those who have been tried and found worthy. Such friends should be carefully nursed back to health. Should this prove impossible, I think the friendship should be not so much broken off or sundered as, to use another's elegant turn of phrase, gradually picked apart. There is nothing worse than open hostilities waged against someone with whom you have been living on close terms. Yet you may well have to suffer such attacks as these on the part of someone you once admitted to friendship, for there are men who render themselves unworthy of being loved by their own behaviour and yet, if something goes amiss with them, lay the blame for it on their friend. The relationship is damaged, they say, and therefore any counsel given them must be suspect. If they are exposed and their offences made public, having no other course open to them, they redouble their hatred and abuse of the erstwhile friend, conducting a whispering campaign, exalting themselves and accusing others with equal mendacity. So if you should be subject to such attacks after the breakup of a friendship, endure them as long as you possibly can, for friendship is eternal, as we read: 'A friend loves at all times.' If he who you love wounds you, love him regardless. Even if his conduct forces you to withdraw your friendship from him, never withdraw your love. Work for his salvation in so far as you are able, have a care for his good name and never betray his confidences, even though he may have betrayed yours.

Aelred of Rievaulx (1109–1167), On Spiritual Friendship

🌸 APRIL 17 🌸

If you ask me 'What makes a man holy?' I will tell you that it is knowledge and love: the knowledge of truth and the love of goodness. You can only come to the knowledge of God and his truth, by knowing yourself; and you can only come to the love of God by loving your fellow Christians.

By diligent meditation you will come to know yourself; and by pure contemplation you will come to know God.

Edmund of Abingdon (1180–1240), The Mirror of St Edmund

🌸 APRIL 18 🌸

God himself, the Bridegroom of the soul, both comes to the soul and departs again at his pleasure, provided that we realize that what is described is an inward perception of the soul and not an actual movement of the Word. For example, when the soul feels an inflowing of grace, it recognizes his presence; when it does not, it complains of his absence and seeks his return, saying with the Psalmist: 'My face has sought you; your face, Lord, will I seek.' Why should the soul not seek him? Having lost so dearly loved a Bridegroom, she will be unable even to think of anything else, let alone desire it. All she can do is painstakingly seek him when he is absent and call him back when he leaves. That is how the Word is recalled: namely, by the desire of the soul, but of a soul which is his, on which he has once bestowed his grace.

'Return' implies a recalling. It may be that was why he withdrew himself, to be called back more eagerly and clasped with greater urgency. For once or twice on earth he made as if to go on, not because he wanted to, but to hear them say: 'Stay with us, for it is nearly evening and the day is far spent.'

For this Word is not irrevocable: he comes and goes as he sees fit, visiting in the morning and, of a sudden, testing. His going is designed to profit us, his return is always of his own free will. The one and the other are weighty with judgment, but he alone knows the underlying reasons.

Bernard of Clairvaux (1090–1153), Sermon 74 on the Song of Songs

❦ APRIL 19 ❦

Seeing that his ways are so wholly inscrutable, you may well ask how I knew that he was present. He is alive and active, and, as soon as he entered in, he roused my drowsy soul. He quickened and softened and ravished my heart, which lay inert and hard as stone. He began to root up and tear down, to build and to plant, to water the dry places and light up the dark corners, to unlock what was tight shut and fan dead embers to blaze, to make the crooked straight and level the rough ground, so that my soul might praise the Lord and all that is within me bless his holy name. So on the occasions when the Word – the Bridegroom – has visited me, he has never made his entry apparent to my hearing, sight or touch. None of his movements has been perceptible to me, nor was it through any of my senses that he penetrated into my inmost being. Only the stirrings of my heart, as I said before, betrayed his presence.

Bernard of Clairvaux (1090–1153), Sermon 74 on the Song of Songs

❧ APRIL 20 ❧

One day when Francis was praying to God to enlighten him, the answer
came: 'Francis, you must despise and hate all that your body has loved
and desired up till now, if you would recognize my will. Once you have
begun, you will find that everything which seemed pleasant and sweet to
you will turn to unbearable bitterness, but the things that formerly made
you shudder will give you peace and joy.'

Thus divinely fortified, it happened that while he was riding in the
neighbourhood of Assisi he met a leper. Up till then he had regarded
such men with great loathing. But lo! now he conquered his revulsion,
got down from his horse, gave the leper a coin and kissed his hand.
And the leper gave him the kiss of peace. Then Francis mounted his
horse and continued on his way.

Giovanni di Ceprano (13th century), The Legend of the Three Companions

❧ APRIL 21 ❧

All the brothers must seek to follow the humility and poverty of our
Lord Jesus Christ, and must remember that we ought not to possess
anything in this world except what the Apostle says: Having food
and raiment, let us be therewith content. And they ought to rejoice
when they are living among common and despised people, among the
poor and weak, the sick and the lepers, and those who beg by the
wayside. And when it is necessary let them go for alms and not be
ashamed.

Francis of Assisi (1181–1226)

❧ APRIL 22 ❧

He [Christ] is the splendour of eternal glory, 'the brightness of eternal
light, and the mirror without cloud.'

Behold, I say, the birth of this mirror. Behold [Christ's] poverty even
as he was laid in the manger and wrapped in swaddling clothes. What

wondrous humility, what marvellous poverty! The King of angels, the Lord of heaven and earth resting in a manger! Look more deeply into the mirror and meditate on his humility, or simply on his poverty. Behold the many labours and sufferings he endured to redeem the human race. Then, in the depths of this very mirror, ponder his unspeakable love which caused him to suffer on the wood of the cross and to endure the most shameful kind of death. The mirror himself, from his position on the cross, warned passers-by to weigh carefully this act, as he said: 'All of you who pass by this way, behold and see if there is any sorrow like mine.' Let us answer his cries and lamentations with one voice and one spirit: 'I will be mindful and remember, and my soul will be consumed within me.'

Clare of Assisi (1194–1253), Letter to the Blessed Agnes of Prague

🐾 APRIL 23 🐾

For [God] brought forth into being in order that his goodness might be communicated to creatures, and be represented by them; and because his goodness could not be adequately represented by one creature alone, he produced many and diverse creatures, [so] that what was wanting in one in the representation of the divine goodness might be supplied by another. For goodness, which in God is simple and uniform, in creatures is manifold and divided: and hence the whole universe together participates the divine goodness more perfectly, and represents it better than any single creature whatever.

Thomas Aquinas (1225–1274)

🐾 APRIL 24 🐾

Upon a certain time when I was at prayer and my spirit was exalted, God spake unto me many gracious words full of love.

And when I looked, I beheld God who spake with me. But if thou seekest to know that which I beheld, I can tell thee nothing, save that I beheld a fullness and a clearness, and felt them within me so abundantly that I can in no wise describe it, nor give any likeness thereof. For what I beheld was not corporal, but as though it were in heaven. Thus I beheld a beauty so great that I can say naught concerning it, save that I saw the Supreme Beauty, containeth within itself all goodness. And all the saints were standing before this beauteous Majesty, praising it.

Angela of Foligno (1248–1309)

APRIL 25

She found herself eager for the next day's Mass – it would be Mary's day – because in communion the soul seems more sweetly bound to God and better knows his truth. For then the soul is in God and God in the soul, just as the fish is in the sea and the sea is in the fish. So when it was morning and time for Mass she took her place with eager desire. From her deep knowledge of herself, a holy justice gave birth to hatred and displeasure against herself, ashamed as she was of her imperfection, which seemed to her to be the cause of all the evils in the world. In this knowledge and hatred and justice she washed away the stains of guilt, which it seemed to her were, and which indeed were, in her own soul, saying, 'O eternal Father, I accuse myself before you, asking that you punish my sins in this life. And since I by my sins am the cause of the sufferings my neighbours must endure, I beg you in mercy to punish me for them.

[The Holy Spirit said:] The infinite sorrow God wills is twofold: for the offence you yourself have committed against your Creator, and for the offence you see on your neighbours' part. Because those who have such sorrow have infinite desire and are one with me in loving affection (which is why they grieve when they sin or see others sinning), every suffering they bear from any source at all, in spirit or in body, is of infinite worth, and so satisfies for the offence that deserved an infinite penalty. True, these are finite deeds in finite time. But because their virtue is practised and their suffering borne with infinite desire and contrition and sorrow for sin, it has value.

Catherine of Siena (1347–1380)

❧ APRIL 26 ❧

[The Holy Spirit said:] Here is the way, if you would come to perfect knowledge and enjoyment of me, eternal Life: Never leave the knowledge of yourself. Then, put down as you are in the valley of humility you will know me in yourself, and from this knowledge you will draw all that you need.

No virtue can have life in it except from charity, and charity is nursed and mothered by humility. You will find humility in the knowledge of yourself when you see that even your own existence comes not from yourself but from me, for I loved you before you came into being. And in my unspeakable love for you I willed to create you anew in grace. So I washed you and made you a new creation in the blood that my only-begotten Son poured out with such burning love.

Catherine of Siena (1347–1380)

❧ APRIL 27 ❧

Very soon the end of your life will be at hand; consider, therefore, the state of your soul. Today a man is here; tomorrow he is gone. And when he is out of sight, he is soon out of mind. Oh, how dull and hard is the heart of man, which thinks only of the present, and does not provide against the future! You should order your every deed and thought, as though today were the day of your death. Had you a good conscience, death would hold no terrors for you; even so, it were better to avoid sin than to escape death. If you are not ready to die today, will tomorrow find you better prepared? Tomorrow is uncertain; and how can you be sure of tomorrow?

Thomas à Kempis (1380–1471), The Imitation of Christ

❧ APRIL 28 ❧

See how in the Cross all things consist, and in dying on it all things depend. There is no other way to life and to true inner peace, than the way of the Cross, and of daily self-denial. Go where you will, seek what you will; you will find no higher way above nor safer way below than the road of the Holy Cross. Arrange and order all things to your own ideas and wishes, yet you will still find suffering to endure, whether you will or not; so you will always find the Cross. For you will either endure bodily pain, or suffer anguish of mind and spirit.

Thomas à Kempis (1380–1471), The Imitation of Christ

❦ APRIL 29 ❦

When he was thinking of those things of the world he took much delight in them, but afterwards, when he was tired and put them aside, he found himself dry and dissatisfied. But when he thought of going to Jerusalem barefoot, and of eating nothing but plain vegetables and of practising all the other rigours that he saw in the saints, not only was he consoled when he had these thoughts, but even after putting them aside he remained satisfied and joyful.

He did not notice this, however; nor did he stop to ponder the distinction until the time when his eyes were opened a little, and he began to marvel at the difference and to reflect upon it, realizing from experience that some thoughts left him sad and others joyful. Little by little he came to recognize the difference between the spirits that were stirring, one from the devil, the other from God.

Ignatius Loyola (1491–1556)

❦ APRIL 30 ❦

So at the beginning of the year '23 he set out for Barcelona to take ship. Although various people offered to accompany him, he wanted to go quite alone, for his idea was to have God alone as refuge. One day some persons were strongly urging him to take a companion, since he did not know either Italian or the Latin language. They told him how much this would help him and praised a certain person highly. He replied that even if the companion were the son or the brother of the Duke of

Cardona, he would not go in his company. For he wanted to practise three virtues – charity, faith, and hope; and if he took a companion, he would expect help from him when he was hungry; if he fell down the man would help him up. He himself, too, would trust the companion and feel attachment to him on this account. But he wanted to place that trust, attachment, and expectation in God alone.

Ignatius Loyola (1491–1556)

MAY

Reflections from Christian Mystics

❦ MAY 1 ❧

The moment in which we become aware of the creative action of God and are therefore able to respond or resist, is the moment in which our conscious spiritual life begins. In all the talk of human progress, it is strange how very seldom we hear anything about this, the most momentous step forward that a human being can make, for it is the step that takes us beyond self-interest, beyond succession, sets up a direct intercourse with the soul's Home and Father, and can introduce us into eternal life. Large parts of the New Testament are concerned with the making of that step. But the experimental knowledge of it is not on the one hand possessed by all Christians, nor on the other hand is it confined to Christianity.

Evelyn Underhill (1875–1941), The Spiritual Life

❦ MAY 2 ❧

The old story of Eyes and No-Eyes is really the story of the mystical and unmystical types. 'No-Eyes' has fixed his attention on the fact that he is obliged to take a walk. For him the chief factor of existence is his own movement along the road; a movement which he intends to accomplish as efficiently and comfortably as he can. He asks not to know what may be on either side of the hedges. He ignores the caress of the wind until it threatens to remove his hat. He trudges along, steadily, diligently; avoiding the muddy pools, but oblivious of the light which they reflect. 'Eyes' takes the walk too; and for him it is a perpetual revelation of beauty and wonder. The sunlight inebriates him, the winds delight him, the very effort of the journey is a joy. Magic presences throng the roadside, or cry salutations to him from the hidden fields. The rich world through which he moves lies in the foreground of his consciousness; and it gives up new secrets to him at every step. 'No-Eyes' when told of his adventures, usually refuses to believe that both have gone by the same road. He fancies that his companion has been floating about in the air, or beset by agreeable hallucinations. We shall never persuade him to the contrary unless we persuade him to look for himself.

Evelyn Underhill (1875–1941), Practical Mysticism

MAY 3

Therefore it is to a practical mysticism that the practical man is here invited: to a training of his latent faculties, a bracing and brightening of his languid consciousness, an emancipation from the fetters of appearance, a turning of his attention to new levels of the world. Thus he may become aware of the universe which the spiritual artist is always trying to disclose to the race. This amount of mystical perception – this 'ordinary contemplation' as the specialists call it – is possible to all men: without it they are not wholly conscious, nor wholly alive. It is a natural human activity, no more involving the great powers and sublime experiences of the mystical saints and philosophers than the ordinary enjoyment of music involves the special creative powers of the great musician.

Evelyn Underhill (1875–1941), Practical Mysticism

MAY 4

I cannot tell you how surprised I was the first time I felt my heart begin to warm. It was a real warmth too, not imaginary, and it felt as if it were actually on fire. I was astonished at the way the heat surged up, and how this new sensation brought great and unexpected comfort. I had to keep feeling my breast to make sure there was no physical reason for it! But once I realized that it came entirely from within, that this fire of love had no cause, material or sinful, but was the gift of my Maker, I was absolutely delighted, and wanted my love to be even greater. And this longing was all the more urgent because of the delightful effect and the interior sweetness which this spiritual flame fed into my soul. Before the infusion of this comfort I had never thought that we exiles could possibly have known such warmth, so sweet was the devotion it kindled. It set my soul aglow as if a real fire was burning there.

Richard Rolle (1300–1349), The Fire of Love

MAY 5

Out of all the various things that clamour for our attention, let us make it our prime concern to love God rather than to acquire knowledge or to engage in dialogue. For it is love that delights the soul and sweetens the conscience, because it draws it away from lesser pleasures and from the pursuit of one's own glory. Knowledge without love does not edify or contribute to our eternal salvation; it merely puffs up to our own dreadful loss. So our spirit must be strong to undertake hard tasks for God's sake, its wisdom spiced with heaven, not the world. It must long to be enlightened with the wisdom of eternity, and glow with that lovely heat which urges us to long for and love the Maker himself; a heat which empowers us to spurn with our whole being everything merely transient.

Richard Rolle (1300–1349), The Fire of Love

MAY 6

Take care that you avoid thinking of anything but himself, so that there is nothing for your reason or your will to work on, except himself. Do all that in you lies to forget all the creatures that God ever made, and their works… This is the work of the soul that pleases God most… Yet it is the easiest exercise of all and most readily accomplished when a soul is helped by grace in this felt desire; otherwise, it would be extraordinarily difficult for you to make this exercise. Do not hang back then, but labour in it until you experience the desire. For when you first begin to undertake it, all that you find is a darkness, a sort of cloud of unknowing… This darkness and cloud is always between you and your God, no matter what you do, and it prevents you from seeing him clearly by the light of understanding in your reason, and from experiencing him in sweetness of love in your affection. So set yourself to rest in this darkness as long as you can, always crying out after him whom you love. For if you are to experience him or to see him at all, in so far as it is possible here, it must always be in this cloud and in this darkness…

Then perhaps it will be his will to send out a ray of spiritual light, piercing this cloud of unknowing between you and him, and he will show you some of his secrets, of which man may not or cannot speak. Then you shall feel your affection all aflame with the fire of his love, far more than I know how to tell you or may or wish to at this time.

The Cloud of Unknowing (14th century)

🌺 MAY 7 🌺

If ever you come to this cloud, and live and work in it as I bid you, just as this cloud of unknowing is above you, between you and your God, in the same way you must put beneath you a cloud of forgetting, between you and all the creatures that have ever been made. It seems to you, perhaps, that you are very far from him, because this cloud of unknowing is between you and your God. However, if you give it proper thought, you are certainly much further away from him when you do not have the cloud of forgetting between you and all the creatures that have ever been made. Whenever I say 'all the creatures that have ever been made,' I mean not only the creatures themselves, but also all their works and circumstances. I make no exceptions, whether they are bodily creatures or spiritual, nor for the state or activity of any creature, whether these be good or evil. In short, I say that all should be hid under the cloud of forgetting.

The Cloud of Unknowing (14th century)

🌺 MAY 8 🌺

When a person is meditating upon God, the grace of the Holy Spirit may move him to feelings of love and spiritual fervour at the thought of Christ's Passion or some other event in his earthly life. Or he may feel great trust in the goodness and mercy of God, his forgiveness of our sins, and his gifts of grace. Or there may come to him a heartfelt fear and awe of the hidden and unsearchable judgments of God and his justice. Or again, while at prayer he may feel his heart detach itself from earthly things, all its powers uniting to reach up to our Lord in fervent desire and spiritual ecstasy. At such times there is no particular intellectual illumination in spiritual matters, or in the mysteries of holy scripture: the person simply knows that he desires nothing more than to pray and feel as he is doing, so great is the joy, delight, and comfort that he experiences.

Walter Hilton (d. 1396), The Ladder of Perfection

❦ MAY 9 ❦

If you wish to make swift and substantial progress along this road, you must constantly bear in mind two things, humility and love. That is, I am nothing, and I want only one thing. Fix the true meaning of these words permanently in your subconscious mind and purpose, so that they will guide you even when you are not thinking of them. Humility says, 'I am nothing, I have nothing.' Love says, 'I desire one thing only, which is Jesus.' When deftly touched by the finger of reason, these two strings, secured by the thought of Jesus, make sweet harmony in the heart of the soul, for the lower you strike on one, the higher the sound on the other.

Walter Hilton (d. 1396), The Ladder of Perfection

❦ MAY 10 ❦

I saw that [our good Lord] is to us everything which is good and comforting for our help. He is our clothing, who wraps and enfolds us for love, embraces us and shelters us, surrounds us for his love, which is so tender that he may never desert us. And so in this sight I saw that he is everything which is good, as I understand.

And in this he showed me something small, no bigger than a hazelnut, lying in the palm of my hand, as it seemed to me, and it was as round as a ball. I looked at it with the eye of my understanding and thought: What can this be? I was amazed that it could last, for I thought that because of its littleness it would suddenly have fallen into nothing. And I was answered in my understanding; it lasts and always will, because God loves it; and thus everything has being through the love of God.

In this little thing I saw three properties. The first is that God made it, the second is that God loves it, the third is that God preserves it. But what did I see in it? It is that God is the Creator and the protector and the lover. For until I am substantially united to him, I can never have perfect rest or true happiness, until, that is, I am so attached to him that there can be no created thing between my God and me.

Julian of Norwich (1342–1413), Revelations of Divine Love

🏵 MAY 11 🏵

As truly as God is our Father, so truly is God our Mother, and he revealed that in everything, and especially in these sweet words where he says: I am he; that is to say: I am he, the power and goodness of fatherhood; I am he, the wisdom and the lovingness of motherhood…

From this it follows that as truly as God is our Father, so truly is God our Mother. Our Father wills, our Mother works, our good Lord the Holy Spirit confirms. And therefore it is our part to love our God in whom we have our being, reverently thanking and praising him for our creation, mightily praying to our Mother for mercy and pity, and to our Lord the Holy Spirit for help and grace.

And so Jesus is our true Mother in nature by our first creation, and he is our true Mother in grace by his taking our created nature. All the lovely works and all the sweet loving offices of beloved motherhood are appropriated to the second person, for in him we have this godly will, whole and safe for ever, both in nature and in grace, from his own goodness proper to him.

I understand three ways of contemplating motherhood in God. The first is the foundation of our nature's creation; the second is his taking of our nature, where the motherhood of grace begins; the third is the motherhood at work. And in that, by the same grace, everything is penetrated, in length and in breadth, in height and in depth without end; and it is all one love.

Julian of Norwich (1342–1413), Revelations of Divine Love

❧ MAY 12 ❧

And sometimes, when she saw the crucifix, or if she saw a man had a wound, or a beast, whichever it were, or if a man beat a child before her or hit a horse or other beast with a whip, if she saw or heard it, she thought she saw our Lord being beaten or wounded, just as she saw it in the man or in the beast, either in the fields or in the town, and alone by herself as well as among people.

Margery Kempe (1373–1433)

❧ MAY 13 ❧

And shortly afterwards she had a great sickness in her head, and later in her back, so that she feared to lose her wits because of it. Afterwards, when she was recovered from all these illnesses, another illness followed within a short time, which settled in her right side, lasting over a period of eight years, all but eight weeks, at different times…

Then she would say to our Lord, 'Ah, blissful Lord, why would you become man and suffer so much pain for my sins and for all men's sins that shall be saved, and we are so unkind, Lord, to you: and I, most unworthy, cannot suffer this little pain? Ah, Lord, because of your great pain, have mercy on my little pain; for the great pain that you suffered, do not give me as much as I am worthy of, for I may not bear as much as I am worthy of. And if you wish, Lord, that I should bear it, send me patience, for otherwise I may not endure it.'

Margery Kempe (1373–1433)

❧ MAY 14 ❧

Ever since I was a girl – certainly from the time I was five years old right up to the present – in a wonderful way I had felt in myself (as I do even now) the strength and mystery of these secret and marvellous visions. Yet I revealed this to no one except for a very few people and the religious who lived in the same community as I; but right up until the time when God in his grace wished it to be revealed, I suppressed it beneath strict silence. The visions which I saw I did not perceive in dreams nor when asleep nor in delirium nor with the eyes or ears of the body. I received them when I was awake and looking around with a clear mind, with the inner eyes and ears, in open places according to the will of God. But how this could be, it is difficult for us mortals to seek to know.

Hildegard of Bingen (1098–1179)

🌸 MAY 15 🌸

And again I heard a voice from heaven instructing me thus; and it said: 'Write in this way, just as I tell you.'

'I, the highest and fiery power, have kindled every living spark and I have breathed out nothing that can die. But I determine how things are – I have regulated the circuit of the heavens by flying around its revolving track with my upper wings – that is to say, with Wisdom. But I am also the fiery life of the divine essence – I flame above the beauty of the fields; I shine in the waters; in the sun, the moon and the stars, I burn. And by means of the airy wind, I stir everything into quickness with a certain invisible life which sustains all. For the air lives in its green power and its blossoming; the waters flow as if they were alive. Even the sun is alive in its own light; and when the moon is on the point of disappearing, it is kindled by the sun, so that it lives, as it were, afresh. I have also set up the pillars that sustain the orb of the earth, as well as those winds which have subordinate wings (that is to say, gentler winds) which, through their mildness, hold the stronger winds in check, so that they do not prove a danger.

Hildegard of Bingen (1098–1179)

🌸 MAY 16 🌸

The first form of humility can be seen in the clothes that we wear, which should be of an appropriate style and clean, and in the place we live.

The second is apparent in the way that we behave towards others, whether we are loving in all circumstances and in all things. This causes the love of God to grow. The third kind of humility appears in the senses and in the way we use and love all things rightly. The fourth form of humility lives in the soul, which is the self-effacing humility, which creates so much sweet wonder in the loving soul. And it is this humility which makes us rise up to Heaven.

Mechthild of Magdeburg (1210–1280)

🐝 MAY 17 🐝

For the more the soul is given from above, the more she desires, and the more that is revealed to her, the more she is seized by a desire to draw near to the light of truth, of purity, of sanctity and of love's delight. And thus she is driven and goaded on more and more and knows no peace or satisfaction; for the very thing that tortures her and gives her the greatest suffering, makes her whole, and what wounds her most deeply, is the source of her greatest relief.

Beatrice of Nazareth (1200–1268)

🐝 MAY 18 🐝

Note whether what enters your mind
Does you harm or good,
Whether it is of the spirit or the will,
There lies the greatest discernment of all.
People think that they are led by the Spirit,
When mostly it is their own will that leads them,
And they regard as consolation from God
What leads them to their doom.

Hadewijch of Brabant (13th century)

The seed of God is in us,
Now
the seed of a pear tree
grows into a pear tree;
and a hazel nut
grows into a hazel tree;

a seed of God
grows into
God.

Meister Eckhart (1260–1327)

The colour of a wall
depends on the wall.

In the same manner
the isness of creatures
depends on the love of God.

Take the colour from the wall and the colour would cease to be.
So too
all creatures would cease to exist
if they were separated from
the love that God is.

Meister Eckhart (1260–1327)

It is good for a person
to receive God into himself or herself
and I call this receptivity the work of a virgin.

But it is better
when God becomes fruitful within a person.
For becoming fruitful as a result of a gift
is the only gratitude for the gift.
I call such a person a wife
and in this sense the term wife is the noblest term
we can give the soul,
it is far nobler than virgin.
Every day
such a person
bears fruit a hundred times
or a thousand times
or countless times,
giving birth and becoming fruitful
out of the most noble foundation of all.

Meister Eckhart (1260–1327)

❦ MAY 22 ❦

All people desire this true celebration of eternal life by nature, for all
people desire by nature their own happiness. But this desire is not
enough on its own: we must strive for God and seek him. Many would
greatly like this foretaste of the high feast to come and they complain
that it is withheld from them. They feel no sublime joy in the ground of
their soul when they pray and, when they cannot feel the presence of
God, they become vexed and pray less often or less lovingly, saying that
they do so because they cannot feel God's presence. This is not what we
should do. We should not do anything less diligently, for God is truly
present with us. Even if we do not know, he comes quietly to the
celebration. And where God is, there is the high feast, and he cannot
refrain or abstain from coming. He simply has to be there when someone
strives towards him and seeks him alone. Though at times secretly, yet
he is always there.

Johann Tauler (1300–1361)

… it would be a great thing for them to have – as do many persons – someone whom they could consult so as not to do their own will in anything. Doing our own will is usually what harms us. And they shouldn't seek another of their own making, as they say – one who is so circumspect about everything; but seek out someone who is very free from illusion about the things of the world. For in order to know ourselves, it helps a great deal to speak with someone who already knows the world for what it is. And it helps also because when we see some things done by others that seem so impossible for us and the ease with which they do them, it is very encouraging and seems that through their flight we also will make bold to fly, as do the bird's fledglings when they are taught; for even though they do not begin to soar immediately, little by little they imitate the parent. Receiving this help is most beneficial; I know.

Teresa of Avila (1515–1582), The Interior Castle

You must have already heard about his marvels manifested in the way silk originates, for only he could have invented something like that. The silkworms come from seeds about the size of little grains of pepper. (I have never seen this but have heard of it, and so if something in the explanation gets distorted it won't be my fault.) When the warm weather comes and the leaves begin to appear on the mulberry tree, the seeds start to live, for they are dead until then. The worms nourish themselves on the mulberry leaves until, having grown to full size, they settle on some twigs. There with their little mouths they themselves go about spinning the silk and making some very thick little cocoons in which they enclose themselves. The silkworm, which is fat and ugly, then dies, and a little white butterfly, which is very pretty, comes forth from the cocoon. Now if this were not seen but recounted to us as having happened in other times, who would believe it? Or what reasonings could make us conclude that a thing as nonrational as a worm or a bee could be so diligent in working for our benefit and with so much industriousness? And the poor little worm loses its life in the challenge. This is enough, Sisters, for a period of meditation even though I may say no more to you; in it you can consider the wonders and the wisdom of our God.

Teresa of Avila (1515–1582), The Interior Castle

🌼 MAY 25 🌼

We cannot know whether or not we love God, although there are strong indications for recognizing that we do love him; but we can know whether we love our neighbour. And be certain that the more advanced you see you are in love for your neighbour the more advanced you will be in the love of God, for the love his Majesty has for us is so great that to repay us for our love of neighbour he will in a thousand ways increase the love we have for him. I cannot doubt this.

It's important for us to walk with careful attention to how we are proceeding in this matter, for if we practise love of neighbour with great perfection, we will have done everything.

Teresa of Avila (1515–1582), The Interior Castle

🌼 MAY 26 🌼

If you are seeking after God, you may be sure of this: God is seeking you much more. He is the Lover, and you are his beloved. He has promised himself to you.

The longing in your soul is actually his doing. You may feel only the smallest desire for him. There may be no emotion about it at all. But the reason your desire rises at all is because he is passing very near to you. His holy beauty comes near you, like a spiritual scent, and it stirs your drowsing soul.

I tell you again – it is not of your doing at all, this moment when your soul awakens. He creates in you the desire to find him and run after him – to follow wherever he leads you, and to press peacefully against his heart wherever he is.

These moments are also ordered of God, and are sent by him in his timing.

John of the Cross (1542–1591)

May 27

Dryness and despair and death will loom again and again, and they will block us like thorns from communion with God.

Again and again, your spirit will want to turn and flee from these, its most terrible and frightening enemies. But the spirit that would grow stronger will let go and deny its own demand for sweetness and comfort. I will go so far as to say that we must turn from 'spiritual gluttony'…

Do we understand that there are only two paths we must choose between? One is to follow Christ through all thorns and learn all that means to deny ourselves and seek God, which will lead us through the death of our old nature and into the light of resurrection life. The other path is to seek the fulfilment of ourselves in God – that is, to seek only the blessings and refreshment of God, but not seek God for himself. This type of spirituality is the enemy of the cross of Christ.

John of the Cross (1542–1591)

May 28

And did those feet in ancient time
Walk upon England's mountains green?
And was the holy Lamb of God,
On England's pleasant pastures seen!

And did the Countenance Divine
Shine forth upon our clouded hills?
And was Jerusalem builded here
Among these dark satanic mills?

Bring me my bow of burning gold!
Bring me my arrows of desire!
Bring me my spear! O clouds unfold!
Bring me my chariot of fire!

I will not cease from mental fight,
Nor shall my sword sleep in my hand
Till we have built Jerusalem
In England's green and pleasant land.

William Blake (1757–1827)

🌸 MAY 29 🌸

This morning I was making my meditation on the 'Imitation of Christ', as I have been accustomed to do this last thirteen years, when suddenly I saw before my inward eyes these words – God Alone. It is strange to say that one sees words, yet it is certain that I see and hear them inwardly, but not in the ordinary manner of sight and hearing; and further I feel how badly my words express that which I experienced, although the remembrance has remained very vivid to me. It was at the same time a Light, an Attraction and a Power. A Light which showed me how I could belong completely to God alone in the world, and I saw that hitherto I had not well understood this; an Attraction, by which my heart was subdued and delighted; a Power which inspired me with a generous resolution, and in some way placed in my hands the means of carrying it out; for it is the property of these divine words to do what they say: and these were the first that God vouchsafed to let my soul hear, and his mercy made them the starting point of a new life. But lo! My God, I have undertaken to tell of thy inward works, and from the first I feel that words fail me. It seems to me that they do not exist to tell of such things… And since it is to obey thee that I write, do thou take care that I fall not into any fault, and give thy poor little creature means of expressing that which is so far above natural comprehension.

Lucie-Christine (1844–1908), Spiritual Journal

✤ MAY 30 ✤

Now that life is almost at an end for us, the light into which we shall
enter at our death begins to shine and to shew us what are realities
and what are not. I love this desert, the solitude; it is so quiet and so
wholesome; eternal things seem very real and truth invades one's soul.
I am very reluctant to leave my solitude and silence for travel. But
God's will be done whatever it may be, not only done but preferred,
adored, loved and blessed without reserve.

Charles de Foucauld (1858–1916), Meditations of a Hermit

✤ MAY 31 ✤

One day during my last term at school I walked out alone in the evening
and heard the birds singing in that full chorus of song, which can only
be heard at that time of the year at dawn or at sunset. I remember now
the shock of surprise with which the sound broke on my ears. It seemed
to me that I had never heard the birds singing before and I wondered
whether they sang like this all the year round and I had never noticed it.
As I walked on I came upon some hawthorn trees in full bloom and
again I thought that I had never seen such a sight or experienced such
sweetness before. If I had been brought suddenly among the trees of the
Garden of Paradise and heard a choir of angels singing I could not have
been more surprised. I came then to where the sun was setting over the
playing fields. A lark rose suddenly from the ground beside the tree
where I was standing and poured out its song above my head, and then
sank still singing to rest. Everything then grew still as the sunset faded
and the veil of dusk began to cover the earth. I remember now the
feeling of awe that came upon me. I felt inclined to kneel on the
ground, as though I had been standing in the presence of an angel;
and I hardly dared to look on the face of the sky, because it seemed as
though it was but a veil before the face of God.

Bede Griffiths (20th century), The Golden String

JUNE

Reflections from the Orthodox Tradition

JUNE 1

True silence is the search of man for God.

True silence is a suspension bridge that a soul in love with God builds to cross the dark, frightening gullies of its mind, the strange chasms of temptation, the depth-less precipices of its own fears that impede its way to God.

True silence is the speech of lovers. For only love knows its beauty, completeness, and utter joy. True silence is a garden enclosed, where alone the soul can meet God. It is a sealed fountain that he alone can unseal to slacken the soul's infinite thirst for him.

True silence is a key to the immense and flaming heart of God. It is the beginning of a divine courtship that will end only in the immense, creative, fruitful, loving silence of final union with the Beloved.

Catherine de Hueck Doherty (20th century), Poustinia

JUNE 2

Deserts, silence, solitudes are not necessarily places but states of mind and heart. These deserts can be found in the midst of the city, and in the every day of our lives. We need only to look for them and realize our tremendous need for them. They will be small solitudes, little deserts, tiny pools of silence, but the experience they will bring, if we are disposed to enter them, may be as exultant and as holy as all the deserts of the world, even the one God himself entered. For it is God who makes solitude, deserts, and silences holy.

Consider the solitude of walking from the subway train or bus to your home in the evening... Consider the solitude of the housewife, alone in her kitchen, sitting down for a cup of coffee before beginning the work of the day. Think of the solitudes afforded by such humble tasks as housekeeping, ironing, sewing.

Catherine de Hueck Doherty (20th century), Poustinia

✿ JUNE 3 ✿

There is no solitude without silence. True silence is sometimes the absence of speech – but it is always the act of listening. The mere absence of noise (which is empty of our listening to the voice of God) is not silence. A day filled with noise and voices can be a day of silence, if the noises become for us the echo of the presence of God, if the voices are, for us, messages and solicitations of God.

Stand still, and look deep into the motivations of life... Stand still, and lifting your hearts and hands to God, pray that the mighty wind of his Holy Spirit may clear all the cobwebs of fears, selfishness, greed, narrow-hearted-ness away from the soul: that his tongues of flame may descend to give courage to begin again.

All this standing still can be done in the midst of the outward noise of daily living and the duties of state in life. For it will bring order into the soul, God's order, and God's order will bring tranquillity, his own tranquillity. And it will bring silence.

At first such silences will be few and far between. But if nourished with a life of liturgical prayer, mental prayer, with the sacramental life of the church, slowly, slowly, like the seedling of a mighty tree, silence will grow and come to dwell in a soul more and more often. Then suddenly, it will come to stay one day.

Catherine de Hueck Doherty (20th century), Poustinia

✿ JUNE 4 ✿

To confuse prayer with solitude, to say that I must have solitude in which to pray, is a fallacy. It is good to have periodic solitude... It is good to gather oneself up, to be awake with the Lord in Gethsemane, to watch not only one hour with him but perhaps more, all along the way of his incarnation and on to Golgotha, on to the resurrection, on to the bosom of the Father and the Spirit.

But this 'solitude' requires only a small place. It can be a room in a large convent or monastery. It can be a place in the attic or the basement of a family house. It may be a part of a room, separated by curtains. That would be a sufficient temporary solitude for simple recollection and greater peace. The daily noises of the street, of the family, of the staff of convents and monasteries would form a gentle reminder that we never pray alone, and never for ourselves alone.

Catherine de Hueck Doherty (20th century), Poustinia

JUNE 5

On the 24th Sunday after Pentecost I went to church to say my prayers there during the Liturgy. The first Epistle of St Paul to the Thessalonians was being read, and among other words I heard these – 'Pray without ceasing.' It was this text, more than any other, which forced itself upon my mind, and I began to think how it was possible to pray without ceasing, since a man has to concern himself with other things also in order to make a living. I looked at my Bible, and with my own eyes read the words which I had heard, i.e., that we ought always, at all times and in all places, to pray with uplifted hands. I thought and thought, but knew not what to make of it.

The Way of a Pilgrim (1884)

JUNE 6

'Listen now, I am going to read you the sort of instruction [*The Philokalia*] gives on unceasing interior prayer.'

He opened the book, found the instruction by St Simeon the New Theologian, and read: 'Sit down alone and in silence. Lower your head, shut your eyes, breathe out gently and imagine yourself looking into your own heart. Carry your mind, i.e., your thoughts, from your head to your heart. As you breathe out, say 'Lord Jesus Christ, have mercy on me.' Say it moving your lips gently, or simply say it in your mind. Try to put all other thoughts aside. Be calm, be patient, and repeat the process very frequently.'

The Way of a Pilgrim (1884)

❧ JUNE 7 ❧

Try to devote every moment you are awake to the Prayer, call on the Name of Jesus Christ without counting the number of times, and submit yourself humbly to the will of God, looking to him for help. I am sure that he will not forsake you, and that he will lead you into the right path.

Under this guidance I spent the whole summer in ceaseless oral prayer to Jesus Christ, and I felt absolute peace in my soul. During sleep I often dreamed that I was saying the Prayer. And during the day if I happened to meet anyone, all men without exception were as dear to me as if they had been my dearest relations. But I did not concern myself with them much. All my ideas were quite calmed of their own accord. I thought of nothing but my Prayer, my mind tended to listen to it, and my heart began of itself to feel at times a certain warmth and pleasure. If I happened to go to church the lengthy service of the monastery seemed short to me, and no longer wearied me as it had in the past. My lonely hut seemed like a splendid palace, and I knew not how to thank God for having sent to me, a lost sinner, so wholesome a guide and master.

The Way of a Pilgrim (1884)

❧ JUNE 8 ❧

After no great lapse of time I had the feeling that the Prayer had, so to speak, by its own action passed from my lips to my heart. That is to say, it seemed as though my heart in its ordinary beating began to say the words of the Prayer within at each beat. Thus for example, one, 'Lord', two, 'Jesus', three, 'Christ', and so on. I gave up saying the Prayer with my lips. I simply listened carefully to what my heart was saying. It seemed as though my eyes looked right down into it… Then I felt something like a slight pain in my heart, and in my thoughts so great a love for Jesus Christ that I pictured myself, if only I could see him, throwing myself at his feet and not letting them go from my embrace, kissing them tenderly, and thanking him with tears for having of his love and grace allowed me to find so great a consolation in his Name, me, his unworthy and sinful creature! Further there came into my heart a gracious warmth which spread through my whole breast.

The Way of a Pilgrim (1884)

❧ JUNE 9 ❧

So I began by searching out my heart in the way Simeon the New Theologian teaches. With my eyes shut I gazed in thought, i.e., in imagination, upon my heart. I tried to picture it there in the left side of my breast and to listen carefully to its beating. I started doing this several times a day, for half an hour at a time, and at first I felt nothing but a sense of darkness. But little by little after a fairly short time I was able to picture my heart and to note its movement, and further with the help of my breathing I could put into it and draw from it the Prayer of Jesus in the manner taught by the saints, Gregory of Sinai, Callistus and Ignatius. When drawing the air in I looked in spirit into my heart and said, 'Lord Jesus Christ,' and when breathing out again, I said, 'Have mercy on me.' I did this at first for an hour at a time, then for two hours, then for as long as I could, and in the end almost all day long.

The Way of a Pilgrim (1884)

❧ JUNE 10 ❧

We all look towards the East to pray but very few among us realize that we are seeking again our ancient native land, the paradise that God planted in the East towards Eden. We make our prayer standing up on the first day of the week (Sunday) but not all of us know the reason: it is not only because, being risen with Christ and being bound to seek the things that are above, we are reminding ourselves, by standing upright on the day consecrated to the resurrection, of the grace that has been given to us, but it is also because this day is in some way an image of the age to come... This day is, in fact, also the eighth day and it symbolizes the fullness that will follow the present time, the day that never closes... the age that will never come to an end. It is therefore necessary that the

Church should bring up her children to pray standing upright on this day, so that with a continual reminder of life without end we should not forget to make ready our food for the journey… The upright posture makes our soul, so to speak, emigrate from the land of the present to that of the future.

By contrast, every time we kneel and get up again we show by our actions that sin has cast us to the ground and the love of our Creator has called us back to heaven.

Basil of Caesarea (330–379)

🌺 JUNE 11 🌺

Know to what extent the creator has honoured you above all the rest of creation. The sky is not an image of God, nor is the moon, nor the sun, nor the beauty of the stars, nor anything of what can be seen in creation. You alone have been made the image of the reality that transcends all understanding, the likeness of imperishable beauty, the imprint of true divinity, the recipient of beatitude, the seal of the true light. When you turn to him you become that which he is himself… There is nothing so great among beings that it can be compared with your greatness. God is able to measure the whole heaven with his span. The earth and the sea are enclosed in the hollow of his hand. And although he is so great and holds all creation in the palm of his hand, you are able to hold him, he dwells in you and moves within you without constraint, for he has said, 'I will live and move among them.' (2 Corinthians 6:16)

Gregory of Nyssa (330–395)

🌺 JUNE 12 🌺

God is known both in all objects and outside all objects. God is known both through knowing and through unknowing… He is nothing of what is, and therefore cannot be known through anything that is; and yet he is all in all. He is nothing in anything; and yet he is known by all in all, at the same time as he is not known by anything in anything.

It is no mistake then to speak of God and to honour him as known through all being... But the way of knowing God that is most worthy of him is to know him through unknowing, in a union that rises above all intellect. The intellect is first detached from all beings, then it goes out of itself and is united to rays more luminous than light itself. Thanks to these rays it shines in the unfathomable depths of Wisdom. It is no less true, however, as I have said, that this Wisdom can be known from every reality.

Dionysius the Pseudo-Areopagite (c. 500)

❧ JUNE 13 ❧

Isaac wanted to bless Esau, and Esau was eager to receive his father's blessing; but they failed in their purpose (cf Genesis 27). For God in his mercy blesses and anoints with the Spirit, not necessarily those whom we prefer, but those whom he marked out for his service before creating them. Thus we should not be upset or jealous if we see certain of our brethren, whom we regard as wretched and insignificant, making progress in holiness. You know what the Lord said: 'Make room for this man, so that he can sit in a higher place' (cf Luke 14:9). I am full of admiration for the judge, who gives his verdict with secret wisdom: he takes one of the humblest of our brethren and sets him above us. And though we claim priority on the basis of our asceticism and our age, God puts us last of all. For 'each must order his life according to what the Lord has granted him' (1 Corinthians 7:17) 'If we live in the Spirit, let us also walk in the Spirit' (Galatians 5:25).

John of Karpathos (?7th century)

❧ JUNE 14 ❧

Has your brother been an occasion of trial for you? Has your annoyance led you to hatred? Do not let yourself be defeated, but triumph over hatred by love. This is the way to do it: by praying to God sincerely for him; by accepting the excuses others make for him or by constituting yourself his defender; by taking responsibility for your trial on yourself and bearing it with courage until the cloud has lifted.

Be careful, if you were praising the goodness and proclaiming the virtue of someone yesterday, not to disparage him today as wicked and perverse, just because your affection has turned to aversion. Do not seek by blaming your brother to justify your culpable aversion, but continue faithfully praising him, even if you are overcome with annoyance, and you will soon return to a wholesome charity.

Maximus the Confessor (580–662)

❦ JUNE 15 ❧

Imagine a circle marked out on the ground. Suppose that this circle is the world, and that the centre of the circle is God. Leading from the edge of the circle to its centre are a number of lines, and these represent the paths or ways of life that men can follow. In their desire to come closer to God, the saints move along these lines towards the middle of the circle, so that the further they advance, the nearer they approach both to God and to one another. The closer they come to God, the closer they come to one another; and the closer they come to each other, the closer they come to God.

Such is the nature of love. The nearer we draw to God in our love for him, the more we are united by love for our neighbour; and the greater our union with our neighbour, the greater is our union with God.

Dorotheus of Gaza (6th century)

❦ JUNE 16 ❧

Humility is the ornament of the godhead. The Word clothed himself in it when he became man. By it he lived among us in the flesh... And anyone who wraps himself in it truly makes himself like him who came down from on high and clothed his grandeur and glory in humility, lest the created world should dissolve at the sight of him. Indeed, the created world would not have been able to contemplate him if he had not taken it to himself and in this way lived within it.

Isaac of Nineveh (d. c. 700)

JUNE 17

What is purity, briefly? It is a heart full of compassion for the whole of created nature... And what is a compassionate heart? He tells us: 'It is a heart that burns for all creation, for the birds, for the beasts, for the devils, for every creature. When he thinks about them, when he looks at them, his eyes fill with tears. So strong, so violent is his compassion... that his heart breaks when he sees the pain and the suffering of the humblest creature. That is why he prays with tears every moment... for all the enemies of truth and for all who cause harm, that they may be protected and forgiven. He prays even for serpents in the boundless compassion that wells up in his heart after God's likeness.'

Isaac of Nineveh (d. c. 700)

JUNE 18

From those who have experience in raising their mind to God, I learned that, in the case of prayer made by the mind from the heart, a short prayer, often repeated, is warmer and more useful than a long one. Lengthy prayer is also very useful, but only for those who are reaching perfection, not for beginners. During lengthy prayer, the mind of the inexperienced cannot stand for long before God, but is generally overcome by its own weakness and mutability, and drawn away by external things, so that warmth of the spirit quickly cools down. Such prayer is no longer prayer, but only the disturbance of the mind, because of the thoughts wandering hither and thither: which happens both during prayers and psalms recited in church, and also during the rule of prayers for the cell, which takes a long time. Short yet frequent prayer, on the other hand, has more stability, because the mind, immersed for a short time in God, can perform it with greater warmth. Therefore the Lord also says: 'When ye pray use not vain repetitions' (Matthew 6:7).

Dimitrii of Rostov (17th century)

❦ JUNE 19 ❧

A man who is deeply wounded in his heart by provocation and abuse shows thereby that deep in himself he harbours the old serpent. If he bears the blows in silence or answers with great humility, he will render this serpent weak and powerless (or will kill it altogether). But if he argues with bitterness or speaks with arrogance, he will give the serpent an added strength to pour poison into his heart and mercilessly to devour his entrails. In this way, daily gaining strength, the serpent will finally devour the very intention of the poor soul to reform and to keep itself reformed by mending its ways of life, and will destroy its power to do so. Thereupon the man will live for sin and become totally dead to truth.

Simeon the New Theologian (949–1022)

❦ JUNE 20 ❧

A man who from dire poverty has been raised to high rank by the king, enriched, clothed in glittering garments and ordained to stand in his presence, looks upon his king with devotion and loves him exceedingly as his benefactor, rejoices in his bright garments, is conscious of his rank and knows the riches bestowed upon him. Likewise a monk who, having truly abandoned the world and all worldly things, has come to Christ and, incited by right emotional perception, has obeyed the commandments and thereby has risen to the heights of spiritual contemplation, contemplates God without prelest and sees clearly the transformation effected in him. For he is constantly aware of the grace of the Holy Spirit illumining him, which is called both a garment and royal purple. For believers, this garment is Jesus Christ himself, since those who believe in him are clothed in him.

Simeon the New Theologian (949–1022)

❦ JUNE 21 ❦

No man, wise in his own opinion, because he has studied all the sciences and is learned in external wisdom, will ever penetrate God's mysteries or see them unless he first humbles himself and becomes foolish in his heart, repudiating his self-opinion together with his acquirements of learning. For a man who acts thus and follows with undaunted faith those who are wise in things divine, is guided by them and with them enters into the city of the living God, and, taught and enlightened by the Holy Spirit, sees and knows things which no one else can see or know. Thus he becomes taught of God.

Simeon the New Theologian (949–1022)

❦ JUNE 22 ❦

A man who loves his neighbour as himself cannot allow himself to possess anything more than his neighbour; so that, if he has possessions, and does not distribute them without envy until he becomes poor and is himself like his neighbours, he does not fulfil the Lord's commandment exactly. In the same way, a man who has a mite or a piece of bread and who sends away a beggar empty-handed, or who, refusing to do for his neighbour what the latter wants, sends him to someone else, is not a man who wants to give to everyone who asks. Thus, a man who gave food, drink and clothes to every poor man and helped him in all other ways, but who disdained and refused only one of them, will still be regarded as one who has disdained Christ our Lord when he hungered and thirsted.

Simeon the New Theologian (949–1022)

❦ JUNE 23 ❦

In purely contemplative prayer, words and thoughts themselves disappear, not by our own wish, but of their own accord. Prayer of the mind changes into prayer of the heart, or rather into prayer of the mind in the heart: its appearance coincides with the birth of warmth in the heart. From now on in the usual course of spiritual life there is no other prayer. This prayer, taking deep root in the heart, may be without words or thought: it may consist only in a standing before God, in an opening of the heart to him in reverence and love. It is a state of being irresistibly drawn within to stand before God in prayer; or it is the visitation of the spirit of prayer. But all this is not yet true contemplative prayer, which is prayer's highest state, appearing from time to time in God's elect.

Theophan the Recluse (1815–1900)

❧ JUNE 24 ❧

May the Lord give you the blessing of a strong desire to stand inwardly before God. Seek and you will find. Seek God: such is the unalterable rule for all spiritual advancement. Nothing comes without effort. The help of God is always ready and always near, but it is only given to those who seek and work, and only to those seekers who, after putting all their own power to the test, then cry out with all their heart: Lord, help us. So long as you hold on to even a little hope of achieving something by your own powers, the Lord does not interfere. It is as though he says: 'You hope to succeed by yourself – very well, go on trying! But however long you try you will achieve nothing.' May the Lord give you a contrite spirit, a humble and a contrite heart.

Theophan the Recluse (1815–1900)

❧ JUNE 25 ❧

Love all God's creation, the whole of it and every grain of sand in it. Love every leaf, every ray of God's light. Love the animals, love the plants, love everything. If you love everything, you will perceive the divine mystery in things. Once you have perceived it, you will begin to comprehend it better every day, and you will come at last to love the world with an all-embracing love. Love the animals: God has given them the rudiments of thought and untroubled joy. So do not trouble it, do not harass them, do not deprive them of their joy, do not go against God's intent. Man, do not exalt yourself above the animals: they are without sin, while you in your majesty defile the earth by your appearance on it, and you leave the traces of your defilement behind you – alas, this is true of almost every one of us! Love children especially, for like the angels they too are sinless, and they live to soften and purify our hearts, and, as it were, to guide us. Woe to him who offends a child.

Fyodor Dostoevsky (1821–1881), The Brothers Karamazov

🧿 JUNE 26 🧿

My young brother asked even the birds to forgive him. It may sound absurd, but it is right none the less, for everything, like the ocean, flows and enters into contact with everything else: touch one place, and you set up a movement at the other end of the world. It may be senseless to beg forgiveness of the birds, but, then, it would be easier for the birds, and for the child, and for every animal if you were yourself more pleasant than you are now. Everything is like an ocean, I tell you. Then you would pray to the birds, too, consumed by a universal love, as though in an ecstasy, and ask that they, too, should forgive you your sin. Treasure this ecstasy, however absurd people may think it.

Fyodor Dostoevsky (1821–1881), The Brothers Karamazov

🧿 JUNE 27 🧿

There is only one way of salvation, and that is to make yourself responsible for all men's sins. As soon as you make yourself responsible in all sincerity for everyone and everything, you will see at once that it is really so, and that you are in fact to blame for everyone and for all things.

Remember especially that you cannot be a judge of anyone. For no one can judge a criminal, until he recognizes that he himself is just such a criminal as the man standing before him, and that perhaps he is more to blame than anyone else for the crime which the man on trial has committed. When he understands that, he will be able to act as a judge.

That may sound absurd, but is in fact true. For if I had been righteous myself, perhaps there would have been no criminal standing before me.

Fyodor Dostoevsky (1821–1881), The Brothers Karamazov

🪷 JUNE 28 🪷

The injunction 'be mindful of death' is not a call to live with a sense of terror in the constant awareness that death is to overtake us. It means rather: 'Be aware of the fact that what you are saying now, doing now, hearing, enduring or receiving now may be the last event or experience of your present life.' In which case it must be a crowning, not a defeat; a summit, not a trough. If only we realized whenever confronted with a person that this might be the last moment either of his life or of ours, we would be much more intense, much more attentive to the words we speak and the things we do.

Anthony Bloom (20th century)

🪷 JUNE 29 🪷

Coming nearer to God is always a discovery both of the beauty of God and of the distance there is between him and us. 'Distance' is an inadequate word, because it is not determined by the fact that God is holy and that we are sinful. Distance is determined by the attitude of the sinner to God. We can approach God only if we do so with a sense of coming to judgment. If we come having condemned ourselves; if we come because we love him, in spite of the fact that we are unfaithful; if we come to him, loving him more than a godless security, then we are open to him and he is open to us, and there is no distance; the Lord comes close to us in an act of compassionate love. But if we stand before God wrapped in our pride, in our assertiveness; if we stand before him as if we had a right to stand there, if we stand and question him, the distance that separates the creature and the creator becomes infinite.

Anthony Bloom (20th century)

First of all, it is very important to remember that prayer is an encounter and a relationship, a relationship which is deep, and this relationship cannot be forced either on us or on God. The fact that God can make himself present or can leave us with the sense of his absence is part of this live and real relationship. If we could mechanically draw him into an encounter, force him to meet us, simply because we have chosen this moment to meet him, there would be no relationship and no encounter. We can do that with an image, with the imagination, or with the various idols we can put in front of us instead of God; we can do nothing of the sort with the living God, any more than we can do it with a living person. A relationship must begin and develop in mutual freedom. If you look at the relationship in terms of *mutual* relationship, you will see that God could complain about us a great deal more than we about him. We complain that he does not make himself present to us for the few minutes we reserve for him, but what about the twenty-three and a half hours during which God may be knocking at our door and we answer 'I am busy, I am sorry' or when we do not answer at all because we do not even hear the knock at the door of our heart, of our minds, of our conscience, of our life. So there is a situation in which we have no right to complain of the absence of God, because we are a great deal more absent than he ever is.

Anthony Bloom (20th century)

JULY

*Reflections from
Christian Poets*

And it was at that age… poetry arrived
in search of me. I don't know, I don't know where
it came from, from winter or a river.
I don't know how or when,
no, they were not voices, they were not
words, not silence,
but from a street it called me,
from the branches of night,
abruptly from the others,
among raging fires
or returning alone,
there it was, without a face,
and it touched me.

I didn't know what to say, my mouth
had no way
with names,
my eyes were blind.
Something knocked in my soul,
fever or forgotten wings,
and I made my own way,
deciphering
that fire,
and I wrote the first, faint line,
faint, without substance, pure
nonsense,
pure wisdom
of someone who knows nothing;
and suddenly I saw
the heavens
unfastened
and open,
planets,
palpitating plantations,

the darkness perforated,
riddled
with arrows, fire, and flowers,
the overpowering night, the universe.

And I, tiny being,
drunk with the great starry
void,
likeness, image of
mystery,
felt myself a pure part
of the abyss.
I wheeled with the stars.
My heart broke loose with the wind.

Pablo Neruda (20th century), 'Poetry'

JULY 2

A pilgrim
travelling on a road where he has never been before
believes every house he sees from afar is the inn;
and not finding it, directs his belief to another;
and so from house to house
until he comes to the inn.
In the same way our soul,
as soon as she begins
the new, never yet made, journey of life,
directs her eyes
towards the goal of her supreme good
and whatever she sees
that appears to have some good in it
she thinks to be it.

Dante Alighieri (1265–1321)

JULY 3

Death be not proud, though some have called thee
Mighty and dreadful, for, thou art not so,
For, those, whom thou think'st, thou dost overthrow,
Die not, poor death, nor yet canst thou kill me.
From rest and sleep, which but thy pictures be,
Much pleasure, then from thee, much more must flow,
And soonest our best men with thee do go,
Rest of their bones, and soul's delivery.
Thou art slave to Fate, Chance, kings and desperate men,
And dost with poison, war, and sickness dwell,
And poppy, or charms can make us sleep as well,
And better than thy stroke; why swell'st thou then?
One short sleep past, we wake eternally,
And death shall be no more; death, thou shalt die.

John Donne (1571–1631), Holy Sonnets

JULY 4

Why dost thou shade thy lovely face? O, why
Does that eclipsing hand so long deny
The sunshine of thy soul-enlivening eye?

Without that Light, what light remains in me?
Thou art my Life, my Way, my Light; in thee
I live, I move, and by thy beams I see.

Thou art my Life; if thou but turn away,
My life's a thousand deaths. Thou art my Way;
Without thee, Lord, I travel not but stray.

My Light thou art; without thy glorious sight
Mine eyes are darkened with perpetual night.
My God, thou art my Way, my Life, my Light.

Thou art my Way; I wander if thou fly:
Thou art my Light; if hid, how blind am I!
Thou art my Life; if thou withdraw, I die…

Thou art the pilgrim's path, the blind man's eye,
The dead man's Life; on thee my hopes rely.
If thou remove, I err, I grope, I die.

Disclose thy sunbeams; close thy wings and stay;
See, see, how I am blind, and dead, and stray,
O thou, that art my Light, my Life, my Way.

Francis Quarles (1592–1644), 'Wherefore Hidest Thou Thy Face,
and Holdest Me for Thy Enemy?'

JULY 5

When God at first made man,
Having a glass of blessings standing by,
'Let us', said he, 'pour on him all we can:
Let the world's riches, which dispersèd lie,
    Contract into a span.'

So strength first made a way;
Then beauty flowed, then wisdom, honour, pleasure;
When almost all was out, God made a stay,
Perceiving that, alone of all his treasure,
    Rest in the bottom lay.

'For if I should', said he,
'Bestow this jewel also on my creature,
He would adore my gifts instead of me,
And rest in Nature, not the God of Nature:
    So both should losers be.

'Yet let him keep the rest,
But keep them with repining restlessness;

Let him be rich and weary, that at least,
If goodness lead him not, yet weariness,
    May tosse him to my breast.'

George Herbert (1593–1633), 'The Pulley'

JULY 6

The seas are quiet, when the winds give o'er;
So calm are we, when passions are no more:
For then we know how vain it was to boast
Of fleeting things, so certain to be lost.
Clouds of affection from our younger eyes
Conceal that emptiness which age descries.

The soul's dark cottage, battered and decayed,
Lets in new light through chinks that time has made.
Stronger by weakness, wiser men become
As they draw near to their eternal home:
Leaving the old, both worlds at once they view,
That stand upon the threshold of the new.

Edmund Waller (1606–1687), 'Of the Last Verses in the Book'

JULY 7

When I consider how my light is spent,
    Ere half my days, in this dark world and wide,
    And that one talent which is death to hide
    Lodged with me useless, though my soul more bent
To serve therewith my Maker, and present
    My true account, lest he returning chide,
    'Doth God exact day-labour, light denied?'
    I fondly ask. But Patience, to prevent
That murmur, soon replies: 'God does not need
    Either man's work or his own gifts; who best
    Bear his mild yoke, they serve him best. His state

Is kingly: thousands at his bidding speed,
And post o'er land and ocean without rest;
They also serve who only stand and wait.'

John Milton (1608–1674), 'On His Blindness'

JULY 8

Happy those early days, when I
Shined in my angel-infancy!
Before I understood this place
Appointed for my second race,
Or taught my soul to fancy aught
But a white celestial thought;
When yet I had not walked above
A mile or two from my first love,
And looking back, at that short space,
Could see a glimpse of his bright face;
When on some gilded cloud, or flower,
My gazing soul would dwell an hour,
And in those weaker glories spy
Some shadows of eternity;
Before I taught my tongue to wound
My conscience with a sinful sound,
Or had the black art to dispense
A several sin to every sense,
But felt through all this fleshly dress
Bright shoots of everlastingness.

Oh how I long to travel back,
And tread again that ancient track!
That I might once more reach that plain
Where first I left my glorious train;
From whence the enlightened spirit sees
That shady City of Palm-trees.
But ah! my soul with too much stay
Is drunk, and staggers in the way.
Some men a forward motion love,

by backward steps would move,
when this dust falls to the urn
t state I came, return.

Vaughan (1622–1695), 'The Retreat'

❦ JULY 9 ❦

irth is but a sleep and a forgetting:
oul that rises with us, our life's star,
ath had elsewhere its setting,
   And cometh from afar:
ot in entire forgetfulness,
nd not in utter nakedness,
railing clouds of glory do we come
om God, who is our home:
en lies about us in our infancy!
es of the prison-house begin to close
pon the growing boy,
   But he
lds the light, and whence it flows,
e sees it in his joy;
Youth, who daily farther from the east
ust travel, still is Nature's Priest,
nd by the vision splendid
 on his way attended;
ngth the Man perceives it die away,
fade into the light of common day.

n Wordsworth (1770–1850), from 'Intimations of Immortality
Recollections of Early Childhood'

❦ JULY 10 ❦

– yet what I am none cares or knows,
ly friends forsake me like a memory lost;
 the self-consumer of my woes,

They rise and vanish in oblivious host,
Like shades in love and death's oblivion lost;
And yet I am, and live with shadows tossed

Into the nothingness of scorn and noise,
    Into the living sea of waking dreams,
Where there is neither sense of life nor joys,
    But the vast shipwreck of my life's esteems;
And e'en the dearest – that I love the best –
Are strange – nay, rather stranger than the rest.

I long for scenes where man has never trod,
    A place where woman never smiled or wept;
There to abide with my Creator, God,
    And sleep as I in childhood sweetly slept:
Untroubling and untroubled where I lie,
The grass below – above the vaulted sky.

John Clare (1793–1864), 'I Am'

❦ JULY 11 ❦

Dear Lord and Father of mankind,
    Forgive our foolish ways!
Re-clothe us in our rightful mind,
In purer lives thy service find,
    In deeper reverence praise.

In simple trust like theirs who heard,
    Beside the Syrian sea,
The gracious calling of the Lord,
Let us, like them, without a word
    Rise up and follow thee.

O Sabbath rest by Galilee!
    O calm of hills above,
Where Jesus knelt to share with thee
The silence of eternity,
    Interpreted by love!

Drop thy still dews of quietness,
　　Till all our strivings cease;
Take from our souls the strain and stress,
And let our ordered lives confess
　　The beauty of thy peace.

Breathe through the heats of our desire
　　Thy coolness and thy balm;
Let sense be dumb, let flesh retire;
Speak through the earthquake, wind, and fire,
　　O still small voice of calm!

John Greenleaf Whittier (1807–1892)

❦ JULY 12 ❧

Say not the struggle naught availeth,
　　The labour and the wounds are vain,
The enemy faints not, nor faileth,
　　And as things have been they remain.

If hopes were dupes, fears may be liars;
　　It may be, in yon smoke concealed,
Your comrades chase e'en now the fliers,
　　And, but for you, possess the field.

For while the tired waves, vainly breaking,
　　Seem here no painful inch to gain,
Far back, through creeks and inlets making,
　　Comes silent, flooding in, the main.

And not by eastern windows only,
　　When daylight comes, comes in the light;
In front the sun climbs slow, how slowly!
　　But westward, look, the land is bright!

Arthur Hugh Clough (1819–1861), 'Hope in the Darkness'

JULY 13

I hear and behold God in every object, yet understand God not in
    the least,
Nor do I understand who there can be more wonderful than myself.
Why should I wish to see God better than this day?

I see something of God each hour of the twenty-four, and each moment
    then,
In the faces of men and women I see God, and in my own face in the
    glass,
I find letters from God dropt in the street, and every one is sign'd by
    God's name,
And I leave them where they are, for I know that wheresoe'er I go,
Others will punctually come for ever and ever.

Walt Whitman (1819–1892), from 'Song of Myself'

JULY 14

The sea is calm tonight,
The tide is full, the moon lies fair
Upon the straits – on the French coast the light
Gleams and is gone; the cliffs of England stand,
Glimmering and vast, out in the tranquil bay.
Come to the window, sweet is the night air!
Only, from the long line of spray
Where the sea meets the moon-blanched land,
Listen! you hear the grating roar
Of pebbles which the waves draw back, and fling,
At their return, up the high strand,
Begin, and cease, and then again begin,
With tremulous cadence slow, and bring
The eternal note of sadness in.

Sophocles long ago
Heard it on the Aegean Sea, and it brought
Into his mind the turbid ebb and flow
Of human misery; we
Find also in the sound a thought,
Hearing it by this distant northern sea.

The Sea of Faith
Was once, too, at the full, and round earth's shore
Lay like the folds of a bright girdle furled.
But now I only hear
Its melancholy, long, withdrawing roar,
Retreating, to the breath
Of the night-wind, down the vast edges drear
And naked shingles of the world.

Matthew Arnold (1822–1888), from 'Dover Beach'

 ## JULY 15

If I might only love my God and die!
　　But now he bids me love him and live on,
　　Now when the bloom of all my life is gone,
The pleasant half of life has quite gone by.
My tree of hope is lopped that spread so high;
　　And I forget how summer glowed and shone,
　　While autumn grips me with its fingers wan,
　　And frets me with its fitful windy sigh.
When autumn passes then must winter numb,
　　And winter may not pass a weary while,
　　　　But when it passes spring shall flower again:
　　And in that spring who weepeth now shall smile,
　　　　Yes, they shall wax who now are on the wane,
Yea, they shall sing for love when Christ shall come.

Christina Rossetti (1830–1894), 'If Only'

Our journey had advanced,
Our feet were almost come
To that odd fork in being's road,
Eternity by term.

Our pace took sudden awe,
Our feet reluctant led;
Before were cities, but between,
The forest of the dead.

Retreat was out of hope;
Behind a sealed route,
Eternity's white flag before,
And God at every gate.

Emily Dickinson (1830–1886), 'Our Journey had Advanced'

❦ JULY 17 ❦

I fled him, down the nights and down the days;
    I fled him, down the arches of the years;
I fled him, down the labyrinthine ways
    Of my own mind; and in the mist of tears
I hid from him, and under running laughter.
        Up vistaed hopes I sped;
        And shot, precipitated,
Adown Titanic glooms of chasmed fears,
    From those strong Feet that followed, followed after.
        But with unhurrying chase,
        And unperturbèd pace,
    Deliberate speed, majestic instancy,
        They beat – and a Voice beat
        More instant than the Feet –
'All things betray thee, who betrayest Me.'

Francis Thompson (1859–1907), from 'The Hound of Heaven'

JULY 18

Upon the sandy shore an empty shell,
    Beyond the shell infinity of sea;
O Saviour, I am like that empty shell,
    Thou art the Sea to me.

A sweeping wave rides up the shore, and lo,
    Each dim recess the coiled shell within
Is searched, is filled, is filled to overflow
    By water crystalline.

Not to the shell is any glory then:
    All glory give we to the glorious sea.
And not to me is any glory when
    Thou overflowest me.

Sweep over me thy shell, as low I lie;
    I yield me to the purpose of thy will,
Sweep up, O conquering waves, and purify
    And with thy fulness fill.

Amy Carmichael (1868–1951), 'The Shell'

JULY 19

No one, not even God, can put back a leaf on to a tree
once it has fallen off.

And no one, not God nor Christ nor any other
can put back a human life into connection with the living cosmos
once the connection has been broken
and the person has become finally self-centred.

Death alone, through the long process of disintegration
can melt the detached life back
through the dark Hades at the roots of the tree
into the circulating sap, once more, of the tree of life.

D.H. Lawrence (1885–1930), 'Fatality'

❧ JULY 20 ❧

Love some one – in God's name
love some one – for this is
the bread of the inner life, without
which a part of you will
starve and die; and though you
feel you must be stern,
even hard, in your life of affairs,
make for yourself at least
a little corner, somewhere in the
great world, where you may
unbosom and be kind.

Max Ehrmann (d. 1945), 'Love Some One'

❧ JULY 21 ❧

The waves run up the shore
and fall back. I run
up the approaches of God
and fall back. The breakers return
reaching a little further,
gnawing away at the main land.
They have done this thousands
of years, exposing little by little
the rock under the soil's face.
I must imitate them only
in my return to the assault,
not in their violence. Dashing
my prayers at him will achieve
little other than the exposure
of the rock under his surface.
My returns must be made
on my knees. Let despair be known
as my ebb-tide; but let prayer
have its springs, too, brimming,

disarming him; discovering somewhere
among his fissures deposits of mercy
where trust may take root and grow.

R.S. Thomas (1913–), 'Tidal'

❧ JULY 22 ❧

Do not go gentle into that good night,
Old age should burn and rave at close of day;
Rage, rage against the dying of the light.

Though wise men at their end know dark is right,
Because their words had forked no lightning they
Do not go gentle into that good night.

Good men, the last wave by, crying how bright
Their frail deeds might have danced in a green bay,
Rage, rage against the dying of the light.

Wild men who caught and sang the sun in flight,
And learn, too late, they grieved it on its way,
Do not go gentle into that good night.

Grave men, near death, who see with blinding sight
Blind eyes could blaze like meteors and be gay,
Rage, rage against the dying of the light.

And you, my father, there on the sad height,
Curse, bless, me now with your fierce tears, I pray.
Do not go gentle into that good night.
Rage, rage against the dying of the light.

Dylan Thomas (1914–1953), 'Do Not Go Gentle Into That Good Night'

JULY 23

Air crowds into my cell so considerately
that the jailer forgets this kind of gift
and thinks I'm alone. Such unnoticed largesse
smuggled by day floods over me,
or here come grass, turns in the road,
a branch or stone significantly strewn
where it wouldn't need to be.

Such times abide for a pilgrim, who all through
a story or a life may live in grace, that blind
benevolent side of even the fiercest world,
and might – even in oppression or neglect –
not care if it's friend or enemy, caught up
in a dance where no one feels need or fear:

I'm saved in this big world by unforeseen
friends, or times when only a glance
from a passenger beside me, or just the tired
branch of a willow inclining towards earth,
may teach me how to join earth and sky.

William Stafford (20th century), 'Grace Abounding'

JULY 24

I came too late to the hills. They were swept bare
Winters before I was born of song and story,
Of spell or speech with power of oracle or invocation,

The great ash long dead by a roofless house, its branches rotten
The voice of the crows an inarticulate cry,
And from the wells and springs the holy water ebbed away.

A child I ran in the wind on a withered moor
Crying out after those great presences who were not there,
Long lost in the forgetfulness of the forgotten.

Only the archaic forms themselves could tell
In sacred speech of hoodie on gray stone, or hawk in air,
Of Eden where the lonely rowan bends over the dark pool.

Yet I have glimpsed the bright mountain behind the mountain,
Knowledge under the leaves, tasted the bitter berries red,
Drunk cold water and clear from an inexhaustible hidden fountain.

Kathleen Raine (20th century), 'The Wilderness'

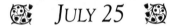 ## JULY 25

Doubt is what you
drown in or walk upon
the solid deck
is never really solid

singing a carol round
the Christmas tree
you can forget that you
are floating but

the ship is not rock-bottomed
all the while
you walk upon the water
I will love

this dark and
downward pulling
angel doubt
that I could never learn

to dance without.

Sydney Carter (1915–), 'Doubt Is'

But he will come again, it's said, though not
Unwanted and unsummoned; for all things,
Beasts of the field, and woods, and rocks, and seas,
And all mankind from end to end of the earth
Will call him with one voice. In our own time,
Some say, or at a time when time is ripe.
Then he will come, Christ the uncrucified,
Christ the discrucified, his death undone,
His agony unmade, his cross dismantled –
Glad to be so – and the tormented wood
Will cure its hurt and grow into a tree
In a green springing corner of young Eden,
And Judas damned take his long journey backward
From darkness into light and be a child
Beside his mother's knee, and the betrayal
Be quite undone and never more be done.

Edwin Muir (1887–1959), 'The Transfiguration'

A gentleness has sometimes stroked my soul
Till the sweetness like angels' sex has spread
From toes to hair and brain, to warm me whole,
And scent me fragrant as the saintly dead.
This never happens in a double bed
Nor at the rail where Jesus' flesh is vended.
No herald of the moment rides ahead;
No chaperone warns that the hour is ended.

We are all women in the hands of God
Claiming *jus omnis noctis* when he will;
He enters, and the sun absents its light
Like a subverted servant, and the night

Curtains the earth and heaven out. When God
Rises and goes, the sweet night trembles still.

Chad Walsh (20th century), 'The Unknowing Dance'

🌺 JULY 28 🌺

Take me, accept me, love me as I am;
Love me with my disordered wayward past;
Love me with all the lusts that hold me fast
In bonds of sensuality and shame.
Love me as flesh and blood, not the ideal
Which vainly you imagine me to be;
Love me the mixed-up creature that you see;
Love not the man you dream of but the real.
And yet they err who say that love is blind.
Beneath my earthy, sordid self your love
Discerns capacities which rise above
The futile passions of my carnal mind.
Love is creative. Your love brings to birth
God's image in the earthiest of earth.

Robert Winnett (20th century), 'Love's Insight'

🌺 JULY 29 🌺

I did not think to find you there –
Crucifixes, large and small,
Sixpence and threepence, on a tray,
Among the artificial pearls,
Paste rings, tin watches, beads of glass.
It seemed so strange to find you there
Fingered by people coarse and crass,
Who had no reverence at all.
Yet – What is it you would say?
'For these I hang upon my cross,
For these the agony and loss,

Though heedlessly they pass me by.'
Dear Lord, forgive such fools as I
Who thought it strange to find you there
When you are with us everywhere.

Teresa Hooley (20th century), 'Christ in Woolworths'

❀ JULY 30 ❀

Prayer is like watching for the
Kingfisher. All you can do is
Be where he is likely to appear, and
Wait.
Often, nothing much happens;
There is space, silence and
Expectancy.
No visible sign, only the
Knowledge that he's been there,
And may come again.
Seeing or not seeing cease to matter,
You have been prepared.
But sometimes, when you've almost
Stopped expecting it,
A flash of brightness
Gives encouragement.

Ann Lewin (20th century), 'Disclosure'

❀ JULY 31 ❀

I shall not see it,
nor the last child born.
nor even yet his son.
Still it will happen,
This is a calculation
you can count on; not

like the railway timetable
that can be disrupted,
cancelled, or run late.

It does not need us,
and we cannot interfere.
If, by that time,
there should be no one
left alive down here
to witness, even so
it will take place.

And knowing this we are
at once diminished, yet
at the same time strangely
reassured, stirred by
the synchromesh of cosmic
gears, as if believing
what has order must have
purpose – as if we sensed
the music of the spheres.

Tony Lucas (20th century), 'Total Eclipse'
The next total eclipse of the sun, visible from London, will be in the year 2142

AUGUST

Reflections from the English Tradition

AUGUST 1

Mistress Alice, in my most hearty wise I recommend me to you.

And whereas I am informed by my son Heron of the loss of our barns and our neighbours' also with all the corn that was therein, albeit (saving God's pleasure) it were great pity of so much good corn lost, yet sith it hath liked him to send us such a chance, we must and are bounded not only to be content but also to be glad of his visitation. He sent us all that we have lost and sith he hath by such a chance taken it away again his pleasure be fulfilled; let us never grudge thereat but take in good worth and heartily thank him as well for adversity as for prosperity and peradventure we have more cause to thank him for our loss than for our winning, for his wisdom better seeth what is good for us than we do ourselves. Therefore I pray you to be of good cheer and take all the household with you to church and there thank God both for that he hath given us and for that he hath taken from us and for that he hath left us, which if it please him he can increase when he will and if it please him to leave us yet less, at his pleasure be it.

Thomas More (1478–1535), letter to his wife, Woodstock, 3 September 1529

AUGUST 2

Dangerous it were for the feeble brain of man to wade far into the doings of the Most High, whom although to know be life, and joy to make mention of his name, yet our soundest knowledge is to know that we know him not indeed as he is, neither can know him: and our safest eloquence concerning him is our silence, when we confess without confession that his glory is inexplicable, his greatness above our capacity and reach. He is above, and we upon earth; therefore it behoveth our words to be wary and few.

Richard Hooker (1554–1600), Laws of Ecclesiastical Polity

AUGUST 3

Repentance itself is nothing else but a kind of circling; to return to him by repentance, from whom by sin we have turned away... which circle consists of two things; which two must needs be two different motions. One, is to be done with the whole heart; the other with it broken and rent: so as, one and the same it cannot be.

First, a turn, wherein we look forward to God, and with our whole heart resolve to turn to him. Then, a turn again, wherein we look backward to our sins, wherein we have turned from God: and with beholding them, our very heart breaketh. These two are two distinct, both in nature and names. One, conversion from sin; the other, contrition for sin. One, resolving to amend that which is to come; the other, reflecting and sorrowing for that which is past. One, declining from evil to be done hereafter; the other, sentencing itself for evil done heretofore. These two between them make up a complete repentance, or a perfect revolution.

Lancelot Andrewes (1555–1626)

AUGUST 4

[The world] think that man hath the gift of Prayer that can utter the thoughts of his heart roundly unto God, that can express himself smoothly in the phrase of the Holy Ghost and press God with most proper words and passionate vehemence. But this is not the gift of Prayer; you may call it, if you will, the gift of elocution... the gift (of Prayer) whereof he may be truly said to have, not that hath the most rennible tongue (for Prayer is not so much a matter of the lips as of the heart), but that he hath the most illuminated apprehension of the God to whom he speaks, the deepest sense of his own wants, the most eager longings after grace, the ferventest desires of supplies from Heaven, and in a word, whose heart sends up the strongest groans and cries to the Father of Mercies.

Joseph Hall (1574–1656)

❦ AUGUST 5 ❦

The number of those who pretend unto salvation, and those infinite swarmes who thinke to passe through the eye of this Needle, have much amazed me. That name and compellation of little Flocke, doth not comfort but deject my devotion, especially when I reflect upon mine owne unworthinesse, wherein, according to my humble apprehensions, I am below them all. I believe there shall never be an Anarchy in Heaven, but as there are Hierarchies amongst the Angels, so shall there be degrees of priority amongst the Saints. Yet is it (I protest) beyond my ambition to aspire unto the first rankes, my desires onely are, and I shall be happy therein, to be but the last man, and bring up the Rere in Heaven.

Thomas Browne (1605–1682)

❦ AUGUST 6 ❦

Pray frequently and effectually; I had rather your prayers should be often than long. It was well said of Petrarch, 'When you speak to your superior, you ought to have a bridle on your tongue'; much more when you speak to God. I speak of what is decent in respect of ourselves and our infinite distances from God. But if love makes you speak, speak on, so shall your prayers be full of charity and devotion. Love makes God to be our friend and our approaches more united and acceptable; and therefore you may say to God, 'The same love which made me speak, will also move thee to hear and pardon.' Love and devotion may enlarge your litanies, but nothing else can, unless authority does interpose.

Jeremy Taylor (1613–1667)

❦ AUGUST 7 ❦

In my younger years my trouble for sin was most about my actual failings in thought, word or action (except hardness of heart, of which more anon); but now I am much more troubled for inward defects and omission or want of the vital duties or graces of the soul. My daily trouble is so much for my ignorance of God and weakness of belief, and want of greater love to God and strangeness to him and to the life to come, and for want of a greater willingness to die, and longing to be with God in heaven, as that I take not some immoralities, though very great, to be in themselves so great and odious sins if they could be found as separate from these. Had I all the riches of the world, how gladly should I give them for a fuller knowledge, belief and love of God and everlasting glory! These wants are the greatest burden of my life, which oft maketh my life itself a burden. And I cannot find any hope of reaching so high in these while I am in the flesh as I once hoped before this time to have attained, which is honoured with so little of the knowledge of God.

Richard Baxter (1615–1691)

🏵 AUGUST 8 🏵

I saw then in my dream so far as this Valley reached, there was on the right hand a very deep ditch, that ditch is it into which the blind have led the blind in all ages, and have both there miserably perished. Again, behold on the left hand there was a very dangerous quag, into which, if even a good man falls he can find no bottom for his foot to stand on. Into that quag King David once did fall, and had no doubt therein been smothered, had not he that is able plucked him out.

The pathway was here also exceeding narrow, and therefore good Christian was the more put to it; for when he sought in the dark to shun the ditch on the one hand, he was ready to tip over into the mire on the other; also when he sought to escape the mire, without great carefulness he would be ready to fall into the ditch. Thus he went on, and I heard him here sigh bitterly, for, besides the dangers mentioned above, the pathway was here so dark that oft times when he lift up his foot to set forward he knew not where, or upon what, he should set it next.

John Bunyan (1628–1688), The Pilgrim's Progress

AUGUST 9

Whensoever we meet together upon a religious account, it is
necessary that the same good and holy things be always inculcated
and pressed upon us, after one and the same manner. For we cannot
but all find by our own experience how difficult it is to fasten
anything that is truly good, either upon ourselves or others; and that
it is rarely, if ever, effected without frequent repetitions of it.
Whatsoever good things we hear only once, or now and then, though,
perhaps, upon the hearing of them, they may swim for a while in our
brains, yet they seldom sink down into our hearts, so as to move and
sway the affections, as it is necessary that they should do, in order to
our being edified by them. Whereas, by a set form of public devotions
rightly composed, as we are continually put in mind of all things
necessary for us to know or do, so that is always done by the same
words and expressions, which, by their constant use, will imprint the
things themselves so firmly in our minds, that it will be no easy matter
to obliterate or raise them out; but, do what we can, they will still
occur upon all occasions; which cannot but be very much for our
Christian edification.

William Beveridge (1637–1708)

AUGUST 10

When I came into the Country, and being seated among silent Trees,
had all my Time in mine own Hands, I resolved to Spend it all,
whatever it cost me, in Search of Happiness and to Satiate that burning
Thirst which Nature had Enkindled in me from my Youth. In which I
was so resolut, that I chose rather to liv upon ten pounds a yeer, and to
go in Lether Clothes, and feed upon Bread and Water, so that I might
hav all my time clearly to myself, than to keep many thousands per
Annums in an Estate of Life where my Time would be Devoured in Care
and Labour. And God was so pleased to accept of that Desire, that from
that time to this I hav had all things plentifully provided for me, without
any Care at all, my very Study of Felicity making me more to Prosper
than all the Care in the Whole World. So that through his Blessing I liv

a free and a Kingly Life as if the World were turned again into Eden, or much more, as it is at this Day.

Thomas Traherne (1636–1674)

❧ AUGUST 11 ❧

Now let any one but find out the reason why he is to be thus strictly pious in his prayers, and he will find the same as strong a reason to be as strictly pious in all the other parts of his life. For there is not the least shadow of a reason why we should make God the rule and measure of our prayers; but what equally proves it necessary for us to make him the rule and measure of all the other actions of our life. For any ways of life, any employment of our talents that is not strictly according to the will of God, are as great absurdities as prayers that are not according to the rule of God.

William Law (1686–1761)

❧ AUGUST 12 ❧

My Dear Friend,
   … if we cannot as yet think alike on all things, at least we may love alike. Herein we cannot possibly do amiss. For of one point none can doubt a moment: God is love; and he that dwelleth in love, dwelleth in God, and God in him.
   In the name, then, and in the strength of God, let us resolve, first, not to hurt one another; to do nothing unkind or unfriendly to each other, nothing which we would not have done to ourselves. Rather let us endeavour after every instance of a kind, friendly and Christian behaviour towards each other.
   Let us resolve, secondly, God being our helper, to speak nothing harsh or unkind of each other. The sure way to avoid this is to say all the good we can, both of and to one another; in all our conversation, either with or concerning each other, to use only the language of love, to speak with all softness and tenderness, with the most endearing expression which is consistent with truth and sincerity.

Let us, thirdly, resolve to harbour no unkind thoughts, no unfriendly temper towards each other. Let us lay the axe to the root of the tree; let us examine all that rises in our hearts, and suffer no disposition there which is contrary to tender affection. Then shall we easily refrain from unkind actions and words, when the very root of bitterness is cut up.

Let us, fourthly, endeavour to help each other on in whatever we are agreed leads to the Kingdom. So far as we can, let us always rejoice to strengthen each other's hands in God. Above all, let us each take heed to himself (since each must give an account of himself to God) that he fall not short of the religion of love, that he be not condemned in that he himself approveth.

John Wesley (1703–1791), from a Letter to a Roman Catholic, Dublin, 18 July 1749

❦ AUGUST 13 ❦

About this time a person at some distance lying sick, his brother came to me to write his will. I knew he had slaves, and asking his brother, was told he intended to leave them as slaves to his children. As writing is a profitable employ, as offending sober people is disagreeable to my inclination, I was straitened in my mind; but as I looked to the Lord, he inclined my heart to his testimony, and I told the man that I believed the practice of continuing slavery to this people was not right and had a scruple in mind against doing writing of that kind: that though many in our Society kept them as slaves, still I was not easy to be concerned in it and desired to be excused from going to write the will. I spake to him in the fear of the Lord, and he made no reply to what I said, but went away; he also had some concerns in the practice, and I thought he was displeased with me.

In this case I had a fresh confirmation that acting contrary to present outward interest from a motive of divine love and in regard to truth and righteousness, and thereby incurring the resentments of people, opens the way to a treasure better than silver and to a friendship exceeding the friendship of men.

John Woolman (1720–1772)

✿ AUGUST 14 ✿

Let not any of you say, this employment is not for me: for it is the duty of 'everything that hath breath'. There is no creature in the universe so afflicted but he has encouragement to pray, and scope for praise some have an idea, that nothing but sighing and mourning are suited to their condition; and that the voice of praise and thanksgiving is for those only who have attained a fuller assurance of their acceptance with God. But they might as well say that gratitude was not their duty, as, that they were not called upon to express their gratitude in the language of praise. Know, brethren, that 'whosoever offereth God praise, glorifieth him'; and, his desire is, that every mourning soul should 'put off his sackcloth, and gird him with gladness'.

Charles Simeon (1759–1836)

✿ AUGUST 15 ✿

Lead, kindly Light, amid the encircling gloom,
    lead thou me on;
The night is dark, and I am far from home;
    lead thou me on.
Keep thou my feet; I do not ask to see
The distant scene – one step enough for me.

I was not ever thus, nor prayed that thou
    shouldst lead me on;
I loved to choose and see my path; but now
    lead thou me on.
I loved the garish day, and, spite of fears,
Pride ruled my will: remember not past years.

So long thy power hath blest me, sure it still
    will lead me on,
O'er moor and fen, o'er crag and torrent, till
    the night is gone,
And with the morn those angel faces smile,
Which I have loved long since, and lost awhile.

John Henry Newman (1801–1890), 'The Pillar of the Cloud'

❦ AUGUST 16 ❦

Ask the saintliest men and women of this world, whether their holy
watch was continuous, and their faith and love as reliable as their
thought; and they will tell you how long, even when they went up
to be with the Saviour on the mount, have been the slumbers of
unconsciousness, compared with the priceless instants when they were
awake and beheld his glory. In every earnest life, there are weary flats to
tread, with the heavens out of sight – no sun, no moon – and not a tint
of light upon the path below; when the only guidance is the faith of
brighter hours, and the secret hand we are too numb and dark to feel.
But to the meek and faithful it is not always so. Now and then,
something touches the dull dream of sense and custom, and the
desolation vanishes away; the spirit leaves its witness with us; the
divine realities come up from the past and straightway enter the
present; the ear into which we poured our prayer is not deaf; the
infinite eye to which we turned is not blind, but looks in with
answering mercy on us.

James Martineau (1805–1900)

❦ AUGUST 17 ❦

And, creeping through the golden walls of gorse,
Would find some keyhole towards the secrecy
Of Heaven's high blue, and, nestling down, peer out –
Oh, not to catch the angels at their games,
She had never heard of angels – but to gaze
She knew not why, to see she knew not what,
A-hungering outward from the barren earth
For something like a joy. She liked, she said,
To dazzle black her sight against the sky,
For then, it seemed, some grand blind love came down,
And groped her out, and clasped her with a kiss;
She learnt God that way, and was beat for it
Whenever she went home…
    This grand, blind Love, she said,

This skyey father and mother both in one,
Instructed her and civilized her more
Then even Sunday school did afterward...

Elizabeth Barrett Browning (1806–1861), from Aurora Leigh

❧ AUGUST 18 ❧

The Spirit of God falls like the dew, in mystery and power, but it is in the spiritual world as in the natural: certain substances are wet with the celestial moisture while others are always dry. Is there not a cause? The wind blows where it lists; but if we desire to feel a stiff breeze we must go out to sea, or climb the hills. The Spirit of God has his favoured places for displaying his might. He is typified by a dove, and the dove has chosen haunts: to the rivers of water, to the peaceful and quiet places, the dove resorts; we meet it not upon the battlefield, neither does it alight on carrion. There are things congruous to the Spirit, and things contrary to his mind. The Spirit of God is compared to light, and light can shine where it wills, but some bodies are opaque, while others are transparent; and so there are those through whom God the Holy Spirit can shine, and there are others through whom his brightness never appears.

Charles Spurgeon (1834–1892)

❧ AUGUST 19 ❧

We sometimes call people irreligious; and, surely, to be irreligious is bad enough: but to be religious is not good enough. A person may be religious, yet not be godly. There are many who are religious; as touching the law outwardly they are blameless: Hebrews of the Hebrews, Pharisees of the straitest sect. They neglect no rubric, they break no law of their church, they are exceedingly precise in their religion; yet, notwithstanding this, they may rank under the class of the ungodly; for to be religious is one thing, and to be godly is quite another. To be godly... is to have a constant eye to God, to recognize him in all things, to trust him, to love him, to serve him. And the ungodly person is one who does not have an eye to God in his daily business, who lives in this world as if there were no God; while he attends to all the outward ceremonies of religion, he never goes to their core, never enters into their secret heart and their deep mysteries.

Charles Spurgeon (1834–1892)

🦋 AUGUST 20 🦋

Death is nothing at all… I have only slipped away into the next room… I am I and you are you… whatever we were to each other that we are still. Call me by my old familiar name, speak to me in the easy way which you always used. Put no difference into your tone; wear no forced air of solemnity or sorrow. Laugh as we always laughed at the little jokes we enjoyed together. Play, smile, think of me, pray for me. Let my name be ever the household word that it always was. Let it be spoken without an effort, without the ghost of a shadow on it. Life means all that it ever meant. It is the same as it ever was; there is absolutely unbroken continuity. What is this death but a negligible accident? Why should I be out of mind because I am out of sight? I am but waiting for you, for an interval, somewhere very near just around the corner. All is well.

Henry Scott Holland (d. 1918)

🦋 AUGUST 21 🦋

You are the block, God is the sculptor; you cannot know what he is hitting you for, and you never will in this life. All you want is patience, trust, confidence, and he does it all. It is very simple – simplicity itself.

John Chapman (20th century)

❧ AUGUST 22 ❧

Do not waste time bothering whether you 'love' your neighbour; act as if you did. As soon as we do this we find one of the great secrets. When you are behaving as if you loved someone, you will presently come to love him. If you injure someone you dislike, you will find yourself disliking him more. If you do him a good turn, you will find yourself disliking him less.

C.S. Lewis (1898–1963)

❧ AUGUST 23 ❧

When we contemplate the physical creation, we see an unimaginable complex, organized on many planes one above another; atomic, molecular, cellular; vegetable, animal, social. And the marvel of it is that at every level the constituent elements run themselves, and, by their mutual interaction, run the world. God not only makes the world, he makes it make itself; or rather, he causes its innumerable constituents to make it. And this in spite of the fact that the constituents are not for the most part intelligent. They cannot enter into the creative purposes they serve. They cannot see beyond the tip of their noses; they have, indeed, no noses not to see beyond, nor any eyes with which to fail in the attempt. All they can do is blind away at being themselves, and fulfil the repetitive pattern of their existence. When you contemplate this amazing structure, do you wonder that it should be full of flaws, breaks, accidents, collisions and disasters?

Austin Farrer (1904–1968)

❧ AUGUST 24 ❧

The simplest thing to be done at this moment is to 'let go' deliberately. In traditional language it was expressed in words like 'Into thy hands I commend my spirit.' If words like these help you to pray at such moments, use them as fully as you can. If you are not accustomed to them or helped by them, find the shortest phrase that expresses for you the entire act of putting yourself into the keeping of the Other. It may be done with such words as 'I/we are in your hands', 'we are yours' or simply reflecting 'let go' while you permit your body to relax. It is probable that we should learn to do this regularly and not just leave it to the times of exhaustion, but if we are going to learn to do it at all, we can begin with those desperate moments.

But it is not easily learned: all of us carry to the point of exhaustion the accumulations of problems and difficulties. Yet praying is a necessary part of truly living, and nowhere is this more true than in respect of the tired, beaten condition which active people find themselves in again and again. To be able to pray 'let go' is so important a part of our life that it deserves all the practice that it requires to become part of our maturing way of living, and its connection with final letting go should not be forgotten.

Alan Ecclestone (20th century)

❧ AUGUST 25 ❧

The question, 'How does God experience me?' suggests a fresh way to look at ourselves and our way of being in the world. What is God's experience of me? God's experience of me must seem strange, disappointing, amusing, hurtful, and occasionally delightful. Once the initial question has been entertained by the believer, its effects go on reverberating in the soul. Because I am capable of reflection and selftranscendence (I can go beyond myself), I can also experience God's experience of me. I can 'see' what I am like from God's point of view. I can learn to know myself in the mirror of God's love, suffering, and joy. When I reflect on how God experiences me I begin to learn more about myself; and the more I understand God's experience of me and my world, the more deeply the mystery of God's passion comes home to me. The making of my soul has something to do with suffering and not just mine and my world's, but God's too. The making of my soul is bound up with the passion for God.

Alan Jones (20th century)

AUGUST 26

Soon, probably in the next decade, the truth would have to be admitted. It would be admitted with a bad grace, be glossed over, softened. And just as we now say 'They burned and drowned witches for a couple of centuries out of a primitive and ignorant terror', soon we will be saying 'When they stopped torturing and killing witches, they locked people with certain capacities into lunatic asylums and told them they were freaks, and forced them into conformity by varieties of torture.'

Doris Lessing (1919–)

AUGUST 27

Two years ago I found myself having to speak at the funeral of a 16-year-old girl who died in our Yorkshire dale. I said stumblingly that God was to be found in the cancer as much as in the sunset... By this I did not mean that God was in it by intending or sending it. That would make him a very devil – yet people are always seeing these things in terms of his deliberate purpose or the failure of it. Why does he allow it? they say, and they get angry with God. Or rather, they project their anger on to God. And to let the anger come out is no bad thing. For so often diseases of strain and depression are caused by suppressed anger and hatred of other people or of oneself. So it is healthy that it should come out and God can take it.

The evidence mounts up that resentments, guilts, unresolved conflicts, unfinished agenda of all sorts, snarl up our lives, and find physical outlet. We do not love ourselves enough: we cannot or will not face ourselves, or accept ourselves. The appearance of a cancer or of anything else is a great opportunity, which we should be prepared to use.

For God is to be found in the cancer as in everything else. If he is not, then he is not the God of the Psalmist who said, 'If I go down to hell, thou art there also,' let alone of the Christian who knows God most deeply in the Cross. And I have discovered this experience to be one full of grace and truth.

John A. T. Robinson (1919–1983)

AUGUST 28

For me the ultimate context in which life is lived is that of an I Thou relationship with the Eternal Thou. That relationship is the umbilical cord of all that one is and all that one does. It seems to me that Jesus lived in the Abba, Father relationship, and that is the ground and basis of all one's being and of all the other relationships that one enters into. Each of these 'others' is a way through which this other relationship comes, both in grace and demand. One tries inadequately to respond to it, but if one is pressed back, then it seems to me that this is the final reality of life, in which and for which one is made. It is not something that begins and ends with what we call time, but it is the framework in which all things of space and time belong and are created and have their being. It is defined in Christ in terms of the love of God and fellowship and grace. It is the centre of everything and it is the context in which one tries to face everything else.

John A.T. Robinson (1919–1983)

AUGUST 29

The Holy Spirit is that power which opens eyes that are closed, hearts that are unaware and minds that shrink from too much reality. If one is open towards God, one is open also to the beauty of the world, the truth of ideas, and the pain of disappointment and deformity. If one is closed up against being hurt, or blind towards one's fellow men, one is inevitably shut off from God also. One cannot choose to be open in one direction and closed in another. Vision and vulnerability go together. Insensitivity also is an allrounder. If for one reason or another we refuse really to see another person, we become incapable of sensing the presence of God.

John V. Taylor (20th century)

✤ AUGUST 30 ✤

If prayer is regarded simply, without qualification, as a rec
do certain things he would not do if we did not ask him a
simply because we ask him, we are wasting our time.

If we are simply wanting something done in a certain si
ought ourselves, no doubt in faith, to be doing something
creative agencies relevant to the subject of our concern. 1
reason to think that God will do 'on his own' what he pur
'with man'. If man will not end war, then, though we pray
will not end it for man.

J. Neville Ward (20th century)

✤ AUGUST 31 ✤

Most people's wilderness is inside them, not outside. Thinki
outside is generally a trick we play upon ourselves – a trick t
us what we really are, not comfortingly wicked, but incapabl
time being, of establishing communion. Our wilderness, ther
isolation. It's an absence of contact. It's a sense of being alon
alone, or saddeningly alone, or terrifyingly alone.

H.A. Williams (20th century), The True Wilderness

SEPTEMBER

Reflections from Lovers of Nature

SEPTEMBER 1

The earth dries up and withers,
the whole world wilts and withers,
the heights of the world wilt.
The earth itself is desecrated by those who live on it,
for they have broken laws, disobeyed statutes,
and violated the everlasting covenant.
That is why a curse consumes the earth
and its inhabitants suffer punishment,
why the inhabitants of the earth dwindle
and only a few are left.

The new wine fails, the vines wilt,
and the revellers all groan in sorrow.
The merry beat of the tambourines is silenced,
the shouts of revelry are hushed,
the joyful lyre is silent.
They drink wine but without songs;
liquor tastes bitter to the one who drinks it.
The city is shattered and in chaos,
every house barred, that none may enter.
In the streets there is a crying out for wine;
all joy has faded,
and merriment is banished from the land.

Nothing but desolation is left in the city;
its gates are smashed beyond repair.
So it will be throughout the world among the nations,
as when an olive tree is beaten and stripped
at the end of the vintage.

Isaiah 24:4–13

SEPTEMBER 2

On another occasion he began to teach by the lakeside. The crowd that
gathered round him was so large that he had to get into a boat on the

lake and sit there, with the whole crowd on the beach right down to the water's edge. And he taught them many things by parables.

As he taught he said:

'Listen! A sower went out to sow. And it happened that as he sowed, some of the seed fell along the footpath; and the birds came and ate it up. Some fell on rocky ground, where it had little soil, and it sprouted quickly because it had no depth of earth; but when the sun rose it was scorched, and as it had no roots it withered away. Some fell among thistles; and the thistles grew up and choked the corn, and it produced no crop. And some of the seed fell into good soil, where it came up and grew, and produced a crop; and the yield was thirtyfold, sixtyfold, even a hundredfold.' He added, 'If you have ears to hear, then hear.'

Mark 4:1–9

❧ SEPTEMBER 3 ❧

'This is why I tell you not to be anxious about food and drink to keep you alive and about clothes to cover your body. Surely life is more than food, the body more than clothes. Look at the birds in the sky; they do not sow and reap and store in barns, yet your heavenly Father feeds them. Are you not worth more than the birds? Can anxious thought add a single day to your life? And why be anxious about clothes? Consider how the lilies grow in the fields; they do not work, they do not spin; yet I tell you, even Solomon in all his splendour was not attired like one of them. If that is how God clothes the grass in the fields, which is there today and tomorrow is thrown on the stove, will he not all the more clothe you? How little faith you have! Do not ask anxiously, "What are we to eat? What are we to drink? What shall we wear?" These are the things that occupy the minds of the heathen, but your heavenly Father knows that you need them all. Set your mind on God's kingdom and his justice before everything else, and all the rest will come to you as well. So do not be anxious about tomorrow; tomorrow will look after itself. Each day has troubles enough of its own.'

Matthew 6:25–34

SEPTEMBER 4

I am the one whose praise echoes on high.
I adorn all the earth.
I am the breeze that nurtures all things green.
I encourage blossoms to flourish with ripening fruits.
I am led by the spirit to feed the purest streams.
I am the rain coming from the dew
That causes the grasses to laugh with the joy of life.
I am the yearning for good.

Hildegard of Bingen (1098–1179)

SEPTEMBER 5

The earth is at the same time
mother,
she is mother of all that is natural
    mother of all that is human,
She is the mother of all,
for contained in her
are the seeds of all.

The earth of humankind
contains all moistness,
    all verdancy,
    all germinating power.

It is in so many ways
fruitful,
All creation comes from it.
Yet it forms not only the basic
raw material for humankind,
but also the substance
of the incarnation
of God's son.

Hildegard of Bingen (1098–1179)

Most High, all powerful, good Lord,
to you be praise, glory, honour and all blessing.

Only to you, Most High, do they belong
and no one is worthy to call upon your name.

May you be praised, my Lord, with all your creatures
   especially brother sun,
through whom you lighten the day for us.

He is beautiful and radiant with great splendour;
he signifies you, O Most High.

Be praised, my Lord, for sister moon and the stars:
clear and precious and lovely
   they are formed in heaven.

Be praised, my Lord. For brother wind
   and by air and clouds, clear skies and all weathers,
by which you give sustenance to your creatures.

Be praised, my Lord, for sister water,
who is very useful and humble and precious and pure.

Be praised, my Lord, for brother fire,
   by whom the night is illumined for us:
he is beautiful and cheerful, full of power and strength.

Be praised, my Lord, for sister, our mother earth,
   who sustains and governs us
and produces diverse fruits
   and coloured flowers and grass.

Be praised, my Lord,
   by all those who forgive for love of you
and who bear weakness and tribulation.

Blessed are those who bear them in peace:
for you, Most High, they will be crowned.

Be praised, my Lord, for our sister,
    the death of the body,
from which no one living is able to flee;
woe to those who are dying in mortal sin.

Blessed are those who are found doing your most holy will,
for the second death will do them no harm.

Praise and bless my Lord and give him thanks
and serve him with great humility.

Francis of Assisi (1181–1226)

❀ SEPTEMBER 7 ❀

Love, divine Love, why do you lay siege to me?
In a frenzy of love for me, you find no rest.

From five sides you move against me,
Hearing, sight, taste, touch, and scent.
To come out is to be caught; I cannot hide from you.

If I come out through sight I see Love
Painted in every form and colour,
Inviting me to come to you, to dwell in you.

If I leave through the door of hearing,
What I hear points only to you, Lord;
I cannot escape Love through this gate.

If I come out through taste, every flavour proclaims:
'Love, divine Love, hungering Love!
You have caught me on your hook, for you want to reign in me.'

If I leave through the door of scent
I sense you in all creation; you have caught me
And wounded me through that fragrance.

If I come out through the sense of touch
I find your lineaments in every creature;
To try to flee from you is madness.

Love, I flee from you, afraid to give you my heart:
I see that you make me one with you,
I cease to be me and can no longer find myself.

If I see evil in a man or defect or temptation,
You fuse me with him, and make me suffer;
Love without limits, who is it you love?

It is you, O Crucified Christ,
Who take possession of me,
Drawing me out of the sea to the shore.

There I suffer to see your wounded heart.
Why did you endure the pain?
So that I might be healed.

*Jacopone da Todi (1230–1306), 'How the Soul through the Senses
Finds God in All Creatures'*

SEPTEMBER 8

A pleasant place I was at today,
under mantles of the worthy green hazel,
listening at day's beginning
to the skilful cock thrush
singing a splendid stanza
of fluent signs and symbols;
a stranger here, wisdom his nature,
a brown messenger who had journeyed far,
coming from rich Carmarthenshire
at my golden girl's command.
About him was a setting
of flowers of the sweet boughs of May,
like green mantles, his chasuble
was of the wings of the wind.
There was here, by the great God,
nothing but gold in the altar's canopy.
I heard, in polished language,

a long and faultless chanting,
an unhesitant reading to the people
of a gospel without mumbling;
the elevation, on the hill for us there,
of a good leaf for a holy wafer.
Then the slim eloquent nightingale
from the corner of a grove nearby,
poetess of the valley, sings to the many
the Sanctus bell in lively whistling.
The sacrifice is raised
up to the sky above the bush,
devotion to God the Father,
the chalice of ecstasy and love.
The psalmody contents me;
It was bred of a birch-grove in the sweet woods.

Dafydd ap Gwilym (14th century), 'The Woodland Mass'

 SEPTEMBER 9

The lopped tree in time may grow again,
  Most naked plants renew both fruit and flower;
The sorriest wight may find release of pain,
  The driest soil suck in some moistening shower.
    Times go by turns, and chances change by course,
    From foul to fair, from better hap to worse.

The sea of fortune doth not ever flow,
  She draws her favours to the lowest ebb;
Her tides hath equal times to come and go,
  Her loom doth weave the fine and coarsest web.
    No joy so great but runneth to an end,
    No hap so hard but may in fine amend.

Not always fall of leaf, nor ever spring,
  No endless night, yet not eternal day;
The saddest birds a season find to sing,

The roughest storm a calm may soon allay.
　　Thus with succeeding turns, God tempereth all,
　　That man may hope to rise, yet fear to fall.

A chance may win that by mischance was lost;
The net, that holds no great, takes little fish;
In some things all, in all things none are crossed;
Few all they need, but none have all they wish.
Unmeddled joys here to no man befall;
Who least, hath some; who most, hath never all.

Robert Southwell (1561–1595), from 'Times Go By Turns'

🌸 SEPTEMBER 10 🌸

　Earth's crammed with heaven,
And every common bush afire with God;
But only he who sees, takes off his shoes,
The rest sit round it and pluck blackberries,
And daub their natural faces unaware
More and more from the first similitude.

Elizabeth Barrett Browning (1806–1861), from Aurora Leigh

🌸 SEPTEMBER 11 🌸

Sometimes, in a summer morning, having taken my accustomed bath, I
sat in my sunny doorway from sunrise till noon, rapt in a revery, amidst
the pines and hickories and sumachs, in an undisturbed solitude and
stillness, while the birds sang around or flitted noiseless through the
house, until by the sun falling in at my west window, or the noise of
some traveller's wagon on the distant highway, I was reminded of the
lapse of time. I grew in those seasons like corn in the night, and they
were far better than any work of the hands would have been. They
were not time subtracted from my life, but so much over and above my
usual allowance. I realized what the Orientals mean by contemplation

and the forsaking of works. For the most part, I minded not how the hours went. The day advanced as if to light some work of mine; it was morning, and lo, now it is evening, and nothing memorable is accomplished. This was sheer idleness to my fellow-townsmen, no doubt; but if the birds and flowers had tried me by their standard, I should not have been found wanting. A man must find his occasions in himself, it is true. The natural day is very calm, and will hardly reprove his indolence.

Henry D. Thoreau (1817–1862)

SEPTEMBER 12

I leant upon a coppice gate
    When Frost was spectre-gray,
And Winter's dregs made desolate
    The weakening eye of day.
The tangled bine-stems scored the sky
    Like strings of broken lyres,
And all mankind that haunted nigh
    Had sought their household fires.

The land's sharp features seemed to be
    The Century's corpse outleant,
His crypt the cloudy canopy,
    The wind his death-lament.
The ancient pulse of germ and birth
    Was shrunken hard and dry,
And every spirit upon earth
    Seemed fervourless as I.

At once a voice arose among
    The bleak twigs overhead
In a full-hearted evensong
    Of joy illimited;

An agèd thrush, frail, gaunt, and small,
    In blast-beruffled plume,
Had chosen thus to fling his soul
    Upon the growing gloom.

So little cause for carollings
    Of such ecstatic sound
Was written on terrestrial things
    Afar or nigh around,
That I could think there trembled through
    His happy good-night air
Some blessèd Hope, whereof he knew
    And I was unaware.

Thomas Hardy (1840–1928), 'The Darkling Thrush', 31 December 1900

🌸 SEPTEMBER 13 🌸

The world is charged with the grandeur of God.
    It will flame out, like shining from shook foil;
    It gathers to a greatness, like the ooze of oil
Crushed. Why do men then now not reck his rod?
Generations have trod, have trod, have trod;
    And all is seared with trade; bleared, smeared
        with toil;
    And wears man's smudge and shares man's smell:
        the soil
Is bare now, nor can foot feel, being shod.

And for all this, nature is never spent;
    There lives the dearest freshness deep down things;
And though the last lights off the black west went
    Oh, morning, at the brown brink eastward, springs –
Because the Holy Ghost over the bent
    World broods with warm breast and with ah! bright wings.

Gerard Manley Hopkins (1844–1889), 'God's Grandeur'

There is religion in everything around us,
A calm and holy religion
In the unbreathing things in Nature.
It is a meek and blessed influence,
Stealing in as it were unaware upon the heart;
It comes quickly, and without excitement;
It has no terror, no gloom;
It does not rouse up the passions;
It is untrammelled by creeds...
It is written on the arched sky;
It looks out from every star;
It is on the sailing cloud and in the invisible wind;
It is among the hills and valleys of the earth
Where the shrubless mountain-top pierces the thin atmosphere of
    eternal winter,
Or where the mighty forest fluctuates before the strong wind,
With its dark waves of green foliage;
It is spread out like a legible language upon the broad face of an
    unsleeping ocean,
It is the poetry of Nature;
It is that which uplifts the spirit within us...
And which opens to our imagination a world of spiritual beauty and
    holiness.

John Ruskin (1819–1900)

SEPTEMBER 15

I rose early and went out into the fresh, brilliant morning, between six
and seven o'clock. The sun had already risen some time, but the grass
was still white with the hoar frost. I walked across the common in the
bright sunny quiet empty morning, listening to the rising of the lark as
he went up in an ecstasy of song into the blue unclouded sky and gave
in his Easter morning hymn at Heaven's Gate. Then came the echo and
answer of earth as the Easter bells rang out their joy peals from the

church towers all round. It was very sweet and lovely, the bright silent sunny morning, and the lark rising and singing alone in the blue sky, and then suddenly the morning air all alive with the music of sweet bells ringing for the joy of the resurrection. 'The Lord is risen', smiled the sun, 'The Lord is risen', sang the lark. And the church bells in their joyous pealing answered from tower to tower, 'He is risen indeed.'

Francis Kilvert (1840–1879)

❧ SEPTEMBER 16 ❧

Flood thou my soul with thy great quietness,
 O let thy wave
 Of silence from the deep
Roll in on me, the shores of sense to lave:
So doth thy living water softly creep
 Into each cave
And rocky pool, where ocean creatures hide
Far from their home, yet nourished by thy tide.
 Deep sunk they wait
 The coming of thy great
Inpouring stream that shall new life communicate:
Then, starting from beneath some shadowy ledge
 Of the heart's edge,
Flash sudden coloured memories of the sea
 Whence they were born of thee
Across the mirrored surface of the mind.
 Swift rays of wondrousness
 They seem:
 And rippling thoughts arise
 Fan-wise
From the quick-darting passage of the dream,
 To spread and find
 Each creviced narrowness
 Where the dark waters dwell,
 Mortally still
 Until

The Moon of prayer,
That by the invincible sorcery of love
   God's very self can move,
   Draws thy life-giving flood
   E'en there.
   Then the great swell
   And urge of grace
   Refresh the weary mood;
Cleansing anew each sad and stagnant place
   That seems shut off from thee,
And hardly hears the murmur of the sea.

Evelyn Underhill (1875–1941), 'High Tide'

🌺 SEPTEMBER 17 🌺

For years I sought the Many in the One,
I thought to find lost waves and broken rays,
The rainbow's faded colours in the sun
The dawns and twilights of forgotten days.

But now I seek the One in every form,
Scorning no vision that a dewdrop holds,
The gentle Light that shines behind the storm,
The Dream that many a twilight hour enfolds.

Eva Gore-Booth (20th century), 'The Quest'

🌺 SEPTEMBER 18 🌺

Sometimes, when a bird cries out,
Or the wind sweeps through a tree,
Or a dog howls in a far-off farm,
I hold still and listen a long time.

My world turns and goes back to the place
Where, a thousand forgotten years ago,

The bird and the blowing wind
Were like me, and were my brothers.

My soul turns into a tree,
And an animal, and a cloud bank.
Then changed and odd it comes home
And asks me questions. What should I reply?

Hermann Hesse (1877–1962)

SEPTEMBER 19

When I saw the wild geese flying
In fair formation to their bases in Inchicore
And I knew that these wings would outwear the wings of war
And a man's simple thoughts outlive the day's loud lying
Don't fear, don't fear, I said to my soul.
The Bedlam of Time is an empty bucket rattled,
'Tis you who will say in the end who best battles.
Only they who fly home to God have flown at all.

Patrick Kavanagh (1905–1967), 'Beyond the Headlines'

SEPTEMBER 20

What a thing it is to sit absolutely alone,
in the forest, at night, cherished by this
wonderful, unintelligible,
perfectly innocent speech,
the most comforting speech in the world,
the talk that rain makes by itself all over the ridges,
and the talk of the watercourses everywhere in the hollows!
Nobody started it, nobody is going to stop it.
It will talk as long as it wants, this rain.
As long as it talks I am going to listen.

Thomas Merton (1915–1968)

SEPTEMBER 21

If you never feel alone,
if you wake up wanting to sing,
if everything speaks to you,
from the stone in the road
to the star in the sky,
from the loitering lizard
to the fish, lord of the sea,
if you understand the winds
and listen to the silence,
rejoice,
for love walks with you,
he is your comrade,
is your brother!

Helder Câmara (1909–), 'If you have a thousand reasons for living'

SEPTEMBER 22

Just as the Earth is unique among the planets and each individual is
unique, so throughout the entire world every individual manifestation of
reality is thoroughly unique. An ancient expression tells us, 'The
individual is ineffable,' beyond all rational understanding. Each oak tree,
each willow, every single life form has its own personality, its own voice,
its own spirit reality. Each communicates its unique mystery that we
never quite comprehend.

How remarkable the creativity of the world about us! Nature never
repeats itself, not in the animal or in the plant world; not in the
snowflakes or the raindrops; not in its geological structures or in any of
its daily displays throughout the observable world.

Our primary response from the human world is admiration – admiration
that is also adoration, since each living being presents to us some unique
aspect of the divine mystery whence all things emerge into being.

In understanding the vast web of interrelations between all natural
phenomena, the flow of energy whereby each reality sustains and is
sustained by all other realities in the entire world, we come to true wisdom.

But the teachings available to us from the natural world are not without paradox. Nature has a violent as well as a benign aspect. There are wind storms, volcanic eruptions, blizzards in winter and drought in summer, floods on the land and tempests at sea. Locust plagues strip the vegetation bare. We might refer to such natural events as the sacrificial dimension of the living world. Within all of them are hidden blessings, attained only by endurance. Only after his struggle with the angel was Jacob blessed.

Thomas Berry (20th century)

❦ SEPTEMBER 23 ❦

It is still the first week in January, and I've got great plans. I've been thinking about seeing. There are lots of things to see, unwrapped gifts and free surprises. The world is fairly studded and strewn with pennies cast broadside from a generous hand. But, and this is the point – who gets excited by a mere penny? If you follow one arrow, if you crouch on a bank to watch a tremulous ripple thrill on the water and are rewarded by the sight of a muskrat kit paddling from its den, will you count that sight a chip of copper only, and go your rueful way? It is dire poverty indeed when a man is so malnourished and fatigued that he won't stoop to pick up a penny. But if you cultivate a healthy poverty and simplicity, so that finding a penny will literally make your day, then, since the world is in fact planted with pennies, you have with your poverty bought a lifetime of days. It is that simple.

What you see is what you get.

Annie Dillard (20th century), Pilgrim at Tinker Creek

❦ SEPTEMBER 24 ❦

The air was palpable with gold
Too brimming for the sky to hold
As burnish'd oak leaves, one by one
Held up a mirror to the sun.
The birds above the fountain rim

Were cherubim and seraphim,
Lifting translucent wings in flight
Against the radiance of the light.
No smallest whisper seemed to stir
The invisible threads of gossamer
Laid on the lawn, yet rainbows ran
Shimmering from span to span.
Midges and gnats with rise and fall
Moved to an ancient ritual
In gauzy dance, O King of kings
It was the hour of humble things!
The small sweet clover magnified
Beheld the bridegroom, was the Bride
And every lowly plantain head
Was haloed by the glory spread!
Then lifting high each shining sword
The grass stood up and praised the Lord!

Josephine Johnson (20th century), 'Evening Prayer'

 ## SEPTEMBER 25

When despair for the world grows in me
and I wake in the night at the least sound
in fear of what my life and my children's lives may be,
I go and lie down where the wood drake
rests in his beauty on the water, and the great heron feeds.
I come into the peace of wild things
who do not tax their lives with forethought
of grief. I come into the presence of still water.
And I feel above me the day-blind stars
waiting for their light. For a time
I rest in the grace of the world, and am free.

Wendell Berry (1934–), 'The Peace of Wild Things'

At start of spring I open a trench
in the ground. I put into it
the winter's accumulation of paper,
pages I do not want to read
again, useless words, fragments,
errors. And I put into it
the contents of the outhouse:
light of the sun, growth of the ground,
finished with one of their journeys.
To the sky, to the wind, then,
and to the faithful trees, I confess
my sins: that I have not been happy
enough, considering my good luck;
have listened to too much noise;
have been inattentive to wonders
have lusted after praise.
And then upon the gathered refuse
of mind and body, I close the trench,
folding shut again the dark,
the deathless earth. Beneath that seal
the old escapes into the new.

Wendell Berry (1934–), 'The Purification'

❧ SEPTEMBER 27 ❧

Perhaps because I was brought up without any orthodox faith, and
remain without it, there was also, I suspect, some religious element in
my feeling towards woods. Their mysterious atmospheres, their silences,
the parallels – especially in beechwoods – with columned naves that
Baudelaire seized on in his famous line about a temple of living pillars,
all these must recall the man-made holy place. We know that the very
first holy places in Neolithic times, long before Stonehenge (which is
only a petrified copse), were artificial wooden groves made of felled,
transported and re-erected tree trunks; and that their roofs must have

seemed to their makers less roofs than artificial leaf-canopies. Even the smallest woods have their secrets and secret places, their unmarked precincts, and I am certain all sacred buildings, from the greatest cathedral to the smallest chapel, and in all religions, derive from the natural aura of certain woodland or forest settings. In them we stand among older, larger and infinitely other beings, remoter from us than the most bizarre other non-human forms of life: blind, immobile, speechless, waiting… altogether very like the only form a universal god could conceivably take.

John Fowles (20th century)

SEPTEMBER 28

Be like a tree in pursuit of your cause.
Stand firm, grip hard, thrust upward, bend to,
the winds of heaven, and learn tranquillity.

Anonymous, Dedication to Richard St Barbe Baker

SEPTEMBER 29

What if there weren't any stars?
What if only the sun and the earth
circled alone in the sky? What if
no one ever found anything outside
this world right here? No Galileo
could say, 'Look it is out there,
a hint of whether we are everything.'

Look out at the stars. Yes cold
space. Yes, we are so distant that
the mind goes hollow to think it.
But something is out there. Whatever
our limits, we are led outward. We glimpse
company. Each glittering point of light
beckons: 'There is something beyond.'

The moon rolls through the trees, rises
from them, and waits. In the river all
night a voice floats from rock
to sandbar, to log. What kind of listening
can follow quietly enough? We bow, and
the voice that falls through the rapids
calls all the rocks by their secret names.

William Stafford (20th century), 'What If We Were Alone?'

❧ SEPTEMBER 30 ❧

The world is our meeting place with God...

If the world, the cosmos, is our point of contact with God, the place
where we join God to work on a project of mutual importance – the
well-being of the body for which we have been given special
responsibility – then it is here that we find God, become aware of God.
This means we look at the world, all parts and aspects of it, differently:
it is the body of God, and hence we revere it, find it special and
precious, not as God but as the way God has chosen to be visible,
available, to us... It is not, then, mere earth or dead matter; it is
'consecrated', formally dedicated to a divine purpose. We do not know
in all ways or even in many ways what this purpose is, but the world is
not ours to manipulate for our purposes. If we see it as God's body, the
way God is present to us, we will indeed know we tread on sacred
ground.

Sallie McFague (20th century)

OCTOBER

Reflections from Christian Women

❦ OCTOBER 1 ❦

So long as women sat with bandaged eyes and manacled hands, fast bound in the clamps of ignorance and inaction, the world of thought moved in its orbit like the revolutions of the moon; with one face (the man's face) always out, so that the spectator could not distinguish whether it was a disc or a sphere… I claim… that there is a feminine as well as a masculine side to truth; and that these are related not as inferior and superior, not as better or worse, not as weaker or stronger, but as complements – complements in one necessary and symmetric whole.

Anna Julia Cooper (19th century)

❦ OCTOBER 2 ❦

Then Hannah offered this prayer:

'My heart exults in the Lord,
in the Lord I now hold my head high;
I gloat over my enemies;
I rejoice because you have saved me.
There is none but you,
none so holy as the Lord,
none so righteous as our God.

'Cease your proud boasting,
let no word of arrogance pass your lips,
for the Lord is a God who knows;
he governs what mortals do.
Strong men stand in mute dismay,
but those who faltered put on new strength.
Those who had plenty sell themselves for a crust,
and the hungry grow strong again.
The barren woman bears seven children,
and the mother of many sons is left to languish.

'The Lord metes out both death and life:
he sends down to Sheol, he can bring the dead up again.

Poverty and riches both come from the Lord;
he brings low and he raises up.
He lifts the weak out of the dust
and raises the poor from the refuse heap
to give them a place among the great,
to assign them seats of honour.

'The foundations of the earth are the Lord's,
and he has set the world upon them.
He will guard the footsteps of his loyal servants,
while the wicked will be silenced in darkness;
for it is not by strength that a mortal prevails.

'Those who oppose the Lord will be terrified
when from the heavens he thunders against them.
The Lord is judge even to the ends of the earth;
he will endow his king with strength
and raise high the head of his anointed one.'

1 Samuel 2:1–10

🥀 OCTOBER 3 🥀

Elimelech died, and Naomi was left a widow with her two sons. The sons
married Moabite women, one of whom was called Orpah and the other
Ruth. They had lived there about ten years when both Mahlon and Chilion
died. Then Naomi, bereaved of her two sons as well as of her husband, got
ready to return to her own country with her daughters-in-law, because she
heard in Moab that the Lord had shown his care for his people by giving
them food. Accompanied by her two daughters-in-law she left the place
where she had been living, and they took the road leading back to Judah.

Naomi said to her daughters-in-law, 'Go back, both of you, home to your
own mothers. May the Lord keep faith with you, as you have kept faith
with the dead and with me; and may he grant each of you the security of a
home with a new husband.' And she kissed them goodbye. They wept
aloud and said, 'No, we shall return with you to your people.' But Naomi
insisted, 'Go back, my daughters. Why should you come with me? Am I
likely to bear any more sons to be husbands for you? Go back, my

daughters, go; for I am too old to marry again. But if I could say that I had hope of a child, even if I were to be married tonight and were to bear sons, would you, then, wait until they grew up? Would you on their account remain unmarried? No, my daughters! For your sakes I feel bitter that the Lord has inflicted such misfortune on me.' At this they wept still more. Then Orpah kissed her mother-in-law and took her leave, but Ruth clung to her. 'Look,' said Naomi, 'your sister-in-law has gone back to her people and her god. Go, follow her.' Ruth answered, 'Do not urge me to go back and desert you. Where you go, I shall go, and where you stay, I shall stay. Your people will be my people, and your God my God. Where you die, I shall die, and there be buried. I solemnly declare before the Lord that nothing but death will part me from you.' When Naomi saw that Ruth was determined to go with her, she said no more.

Ruth 1:3–18

🎔 OCTOBER 4 🎔

Soon afterwards Mary set out and hurried away to a town in the uplands of Judah. She went into Zechariah's house and greeted Elizabeth. And when Elizabeth heard Mary's greeting, the baby stirred in her womb. Then Elizabeth was filled with the Holy Spirit and exclaimed in a loud voice, 'God's blessing is on you above all women, and his blessing is on the fruit of your womb. Who am I, that the mother of my Lord should visit me? I tell you, when your greeting sounded in my ears, the baby in my womb leapt for joy. Happy is she who has had faith that the Lord's promise to her would be fulfilled!'

And Mary said:

'My soul tells out the greatness of the Lord,
my spirit has rejoiced in God my Saviour;
for he has looked with favour on his servant,
lowly as she is.
From this day forward
all generations will count me blessed,
for the Mighty God has done great things for me.
His name is holy,

his mercy sure from generation to generation
towards those who fear him.
He has shown the might of his arm,
he has routed the proud and all their schemes;
he has brought down monarchs from their thrones,
and raised on high the lowly.
He has filled the hungry with good things,
and sent the rich away empty.
He has come to the help of Israel his servant,
as he promised to our forefathers;
he has not forgotten to show mercy
to Abraham and his children's children for ever.'

Luke 1:39–55

OCTOBER 5

At a time when she was well and twenty-four years old she dreamed that she was pregnant with our Lord. She was so filled with grace that every part of her body felt this grace. And she experienced such tenderness towards the child that she had to guard herself for his sake… And after a while she dreamed that she gave birth to him without any pain and she experienced such extraordinary joy that after she had carried it within her for a while she felt she could no longer deny it and so she took the child in her arms and brought it before all those assembled in the refectory and said, 'Rejoice with me… I conceived Jesu and now have given birth to him' and she showed them the child and when she was full of joy as she walked around with him, she awoke.

Christina Ebner (1277–1356)

OCTOBER 6

For are you not my mother and more than my mother? The mother who bore me laboured in delivering me for one day or one night but you, my sweet and lovely Lord, laboured for me for more than thirty years. Ah…

with what love you laboured for me and bore me through your whole life. But when the time approached for you to be delivered, your labour pains were so great that your holy sweat was like great drops of blood that came out of your body and fell on the earth… when the hour of your delivery came you were placed on the hard bed of the cross… and your nerves and all your veins were broken. And truly it is no surprise that your veins burst when in one day you gave birth to the whole world.

Marguerite d'Oingt (b. 1310)

🌼 OCTOBER 7 🌼

There Adam slept, and God formed the body of woman from one of his ribs, signifying that she should stand at his side as a companion and never lie at his feet like a slave, and also that he should love her as his own flesh… I don't know if you have already noted this: she was created in the image of God. How can any mouth dare to slander the vessel which bears such a holy imprint?… God created the soul and placed wholly similar souls, equally good and noble, in the feminine and masculine bodies… [W]oman was made by the Supreme Craftsman. In what place was she created? In the Terrestrial Paradise. From what substance? Was it vile matter? No, it was the noblest substance which had ever been created: it was from the body of man which God made woman.

Christine de Pizan (1365–1430)

🌼 OCTOBER 8 🌼

Will my spirit dare speak out
and name you father? Yes, and ours:
This you have permitted in the Our Father…
But Lord, if you are my Father
May I think that I am your Mother?
To engender you by whom I am created:
This is a mystery I cannot comprehend:
But you ended my doubt

When, in preaching, stretching forth your arms
You said: 'Those who do the will of my Father
Are my brothers, and my sisters, and my mother.'

Marguerite d'Angouleme (1492–1549)

🕮 OCTOBER 9 🕮

You are women and a woman is always a beautiful thing. You have been
dragged deep in the mud; but still you are women. God calls to you, as
he did to Zion long ago, 'Awake, awake! Thou that sittest in the dust,
put on thy beautiful garments.' You can be the friend and companion of
him who came to seek and to save that which was lost. Fractures well
healed make us more strong. Take of the very stones over which you
have stumbled and fallen, and use them to pave your road to heaven.

Josephine Butler (1828–1906)

🕮 OCTOBER 10 🕮

Because we cannot see the hand of God in our affairs, we rush to the
conclusion that he has lost sight of them and of us. We look at the
'seemings' of things instead of at the underlying facts, and declare that,
because God is unseen, he must necessarily be absent. And especially is
this the case if we are conscious of having ourselves wandered away
from him and forgotten him. We judge him by ourselves, and think that
he must also have forgotten and forsaken us. We measure his truth by
our falseness, and find it hard to believe he can be faithful when we
know ourselves to be so unfaithful.

Hannah Whitall Smith (20th century)

🕮 OCTOBER 11 🕮

Think rather of the high noon of summer, or the stillness of a snow-
covered country, how the heat or lightness everywhere gives an intense

sense of overflowing and abounding life, making a quietness of rapture rather than of fear. Such, only of a deeper and far more intimate kind, is the atmosphere of waiting souls. It may be that words will spring out of these depths, it may be that vocal prayer or praise shall flow forth at the bidding of him whose presence makes worship a communion, but whether there be speech or silence matters not. Gradually, as mind, soul, and even body grow still, sinking deeper and deeper into the life of God, the pettinesses, the tangles, the failures of the outer life begin to be seen in their true proportions, and the sense of the divine infilling, uplifting, redeeming Love becomes real and illuminating. Things are seen and known that are hidden to the ordinary faculties. This state is not merely one of quiescence; the soul is alive, active, vigorous, yet so still that it hardly knows how intense is its own vital action.

Joan Mary Fry (20th century)

❧ OCTOBER 12 ❧

I'm ceded – I've stopped being Theirs –
The name They dropped upon my face
With water, in the country church
Is finished using, now,
And They can put it with my Dolls,
My childhood, and the strings of spools,
I've finished threading – too –

Baptized, before, without the choice,
But this time, consciously, of Grace –
Unto supremest name –
Called to my Full – The Crescent dropped –
Existence's whole Arc, filled up,
With one small Diadem.

My second Rank – too small the first –
Crowned – Crowing – on my Father's breast –
A half unconscious Queen –
But this time – Adequate – Erect,

With Will to choose, or to reject,
And I choose, just a Crown –

Emily Dickinson (1830–1886)

❋ OCTOBER 13 ❋

I have always desired to become a saint, but in comparing myself with
the saints I have always felt that I am as far removed from them as a
grain of sand, trampled underfoot by the passer-by, is from the mountain
whose summit is lost in the clouds.

Instead of feeling discouraged by such reflections, I concluded that God
would not inspire a wish which could not be realized, and that in spite of
my littleness I might aim to become a saint. 'It is impossible', I said, 'for me
to become great, so I must bear with myself and my many imperfections'.

But I will seek out a means of reaching heaven by a little way – very
short, very straight and entirely new. We live in an age of inventions.
There are lifts which save us the trouble of climbing stairs.

I will try to find a lift by which I may be raised to God, for I am too
small to climb the steep stairway of perfection.

Thérèse of Lisieux (1873–1897)

❋ OCTOBER 14 ❋

Some time ago I was watching the flicker, almost imperceptible, of a tiny
night-light. One of the sisters came up and, having lit her own candle in
the dying flame, passed it round to light the candles of the others. And
the thought came to me: 'Who dares glory in their own good works? It
needs but one faint spark to set the world on fire.'

We come in touch with burning and shining lights, set high on the
candlestick of the Church, and we think we are receiving from them
grace and light. But from where do they borrow their fire?

Very possibly from the prayers of some devout and hidden soul
whose inward shining is not apparent to human eyes – some soul of
unrecognized virtue, and in her own sight of little worth: a dying flame!

What mysteries we shall one day see unveiled! I have often thought that perhaps I owe all the graces with which I am laden to some little soul whom I shall know only in heaven.

Thérèse of Lisieux (1873–1897)

❦ OCTOBER 15 ❦

There is a daily round for beauty as well as for goodness, a world of flowers and books and cinemas and clothes and manners as well as of mountains and masterpieces. God is in all beauty, not only in the natural beauty of earth and sky, but in all fitness of language and rhythm, whether it describe a heavenly vision or a street fight, a Hamlet or a Falstaff, a philosophy or a joke; in all fitness of line and colour and shade, whether seen in the Sistine Madonna or a child's knitted frock; in all fitness of sound and beat and measure, whether the result be Bach's Passion music or a nursery jingle. The quantity of God, so to speak, varies in the different examples, but his quality of beauty in fitness remains the same.

Caroline C. Graveson (20th century)

❦ OCTOBER 16 ❦

Art, as is true of all of man's profound experiences, is not for art's sake, nor for religion's sake, nor for the sake of beauty nor for any 'cause'. Art is for man's sake. It may be for one man's sake, or two billion. It may be for man today or man a hundred years from now. No matter.

But the artist is never alone. He has an intimate relationship with the wood he is carving, the paint and canvas, the words, the stone: these are making their demands and their plea and offering their gifts and he is answering and the dialogue sustains him – as do another man's beliefs and memories and the knowledge that there are those who care. The artist knows something else, wordless, oftentimes, but he knows it deep within him: that were it not for the struggle and the loneliness he undergoes in his search for integrity there would be no strength or beauty in his work. (And though art is not for the sake of beauty, beauty must be there or the profound revelation the artist makes would be unbearable.)

The artist in us knows, the poet in us knows: it is the mark not of ordeal but of mastered ordeal that gives a face, a life, a great event, or a great work of art its style. The wound is there but the triumph also, the death and the birth, the pain and the deep satisfactions: it is all there in delicate equilibrium, speaking to us.

Lillian Smith (1897–1966)

 OCTOBER 17

I was lonely, dead lonely. And I was to find out then, as I found out so many times, over and over again, that women especially are social beings, who are not content with just husband and family, but must have a community, a group, and exchange with others... Young and old, even in the busiest years of our lives, we women especially are victims of the long loneliness.

Dorothy Day (20th century)

OCTOBER 18

What of those many loving people who do not find God? Are they in this world deprived of Christ? I think the answer is again in the cross. Wherever there is suffering, there they find him, and with or without recognition that is always where the greatest men and women do find him. Francis of Assisi, Father Damian, Elizabeth Fry, Albert Schweitzer, these and many other Christians knew that they found Christ in those whom they served and acknowledged that the love they felt was God's love in them, but those who do not know do the same work for the same God and have a richness and fulfilment in their lives unknown to many so-called Christians. I know of one, a man who has suffered the impossible things, war, grief, torture and imprisonment, and come through uncorrupted, with a compassion so strong that wherever he may be in the world he must find his way to those who suffer most, no matter how terrible their suffering or how dreadful the place where they are, and keep them company, and serve them as far as he is able.

Elizabeth Goudge (1900–1984)

🎴 OCTOBER 19 🎴

I remember now that I did accept, that night when I woke up in the hospital room… and I realized that I was sane again. I was so thankful that I said, yes, I'll do it. You might say that wasn't a real acceptance because what I'd refused had already happened to me. But yet it was. You can go on refusing even after it's happened to you, like the child who screams and kicks the door after it's been shut up in the dark room. Or you can sit quietly down in the dark and watch for the return of light.

Elizabeth Goudge (1900–1984), The Scent of Water

🎴 OCTOBER 20 🎴

Perhaps it is no wonder that women were first at the Cradle and last at the Cross. They had never known a man like this man – there has never been such another. A Prophet and teacher who never nagged at them, never flattered or coaxed or patronized; who never made arch jokes about them, never treated them either as 'The women, God help us' or 'The ladies, God bless them!'; who rebuked without querulousness and praised without condescension; who took their questions and arguments seriously; who never mapped out their sphere for them, never urged them to be feminine or jeered at them for being female; who had no axe to grind and no uneasy male dignity to defend; who took them as he found them and was completely unselfconscious. There is no act, no sermon, no parable in the whole Gospel that borrows its pungency from female perversity; nobody could possibly guess from the words and deeds of Jesus that there was anything 'funny' about woman's nature.

But we might easily deduce it from his contemporaries, and from his prophets before him, and from his Church to this day. Women are not human; nobody shall persuade us that they are human; let them say what they like, we will not believe it, though One rose from the dead.

Dorothy L. Sayers (1893–1957)

OCTOBER 21

The desert waits,
ready for those who come,
who come obedient to the Spirit's leading;
or who are driven,
because they will not come any other way.

The desert always waits,
ready to let us know who we are
the place of self-discovery.

And whilst we fear, and rightly,
the loneliness and emptiness and harshness,
we forget the angels,
whom we cannot see for our blindness,
but who come when God decides
that we need their help;
when we are ready
for what they can give us.

Ruth Burgess (20th century), 'The Desert'

OCTOBER 22

And you held me and there were no words
and there was no time and you held me
and there was only wanting and
being held and being filled with wanting
and I was nothing but letting go
and being held
and there were no words and there
needed to be no words

and there was no terror only stillness
and I was wanting nothing and
it was fullness and it was like aching for God
and it was touch and warmth and
darkness and no time and no words and we flowed
and I flowed and I was not empty
and I was given up to the dark and
in the darkness I was not lost
and the wanting was like fullness and I could
hardly hold it and I was held and
you were dark and warm and without time and
without words and you held me.

Janet Morley (20th century), 'And You Held Me'

OCTOBER 23

Terrified we see. It is terrible, what we see. And it is good that we see together that we are not alone. We see broken body-selves crying to be healed, separated people, yearning for relation; suffering humanity raging for justice; nations, strangers, friends, spouses, lovers, children, sisters, brothers with us, we begin to remember ourselves, compelled by a power in relation that is relentless in its determination to break through the boundaries and boxes that separate us. We are driven back to speak the Word that spills among us: 'Without our touching there is no God. Without our relation, there is no God. Without our crying, our yearning, our raging, there is no God. For in the beginning is the relation, and in the relation is the power that creates the world, through us, and with us, and by us, you and I, you and we, and none of us alone.'

Carter Heyward (20th century)

OCTOBER 24

It was only after the sense of Presence left me that I recognized its existence and importance in my life. Of course I thought the sense of

Presence left me because I had done something wrong. It never occurred to me that I was embarking on a new stage of my inner life; rather it seemed as if my inner life was now over, that perhaps it had been a delusion in the first place. I only knew that I was in pain, that I could not pray in my usual way (or any way at all), that reading scripture was dry and repulsive to me, and that it was painful to go to Mass and the sacraments.

An anonymous woman

OCTOBER 25

I'm still struggling. To love one's neighbour as oneself presupposes love of self. Real love is built on integrity and justice, not door-mat servility. But there is a precarious balance. I struggle to believe it is OK to pay attention to myself, but I am also wary of the siren song of overdoing self-awareness, self-service, consciousness raising, and neglecting legitimate forms of self-denial in my family...

That conflict was a great struggle particularly last year when I began the spiritual direction that began against everything I was brought up on. I was helped to see that it was a matter of life and death for me. So I undertook it as a project in healing, in reclaiming my body / being. The conflict still rears its head but I have come to believe I can't be for others unless I take care of myself and set some limits. I think the conflict will always be there. I am trying to grow in my ability to be in touch with who I am and to be able to discern in that light the appropriate thing to do for my own being.

Two anonymous women

OCTOBER 26

You have both the freedom and the responsibility to care about yourself. You have the right to think and feel and make choices and changes. Consider thinking about yourself in new ways:

I am not to blame for being beaten and abused.
I am not the cause of another's violent behaviour.

I do not like it or want it.
I am an important human being.
I am a worthwhile woman.
I deserve to be treated with respect.
I do have power over my own life.
I can use my power to take good care of myself.
I can decide for myself what is best for me.
I can make changes in my life if I want to.
I am not alone. I can ask others to help me.
I am worth working for and changing for.
I deserve to make my own life safe and happy.

Jennifer Baker Fleming (20th century)

OCTOBER 27

It is very easy to believe in the indwelling presence of Christ in the souls of imaginary people; to believe in it in people whom we do not know; but it is very difficult in the case of our own relations and our intimate friends.

Somehow it is difficult to believe that the Holy Spirit abides in people who are not picturesque. When we think of Christ in the workman, we think of him in a special kind of workman who wears an open shirt and is assisted in carrying the burden of social injustice by a truly magnificent physique. We do not think of him in the man who delivers the milk or calls to mend the pipes. We do not think of him in the porters in the apartment houses. Recently, in a big block, a frail little porter fell down dead. Everyone agreed that the heavy luggage he had been in the habit of carrying for the tenants was too much for him, though only after a post mortem was it realized. No one was struck by the idea that in this little man a scene from the Passion had been lived again; he had fallen under the weight of the cross.

It is easy to believe in Christ in the refugee when he is on the road, easy to believe when the refugee mother arrives at an English port, with a shawl round her head and a baby in her arms; but how hard to believe in the presence of God in the same refugees when they have got good work, are housed and fed, and possess hats and gloves.

Caryll Houselander (1901–1954)

OCTOBER 28

Moon shell, who named you? Some intuitive woman I like to think. I shall give you another name – Island shell. I cannot live for ever on my island. But I can take you back to my desk in Connecticut. You will sit there and fasten your single eye upon me. You will make me think, with your smooth circles winding inward to the tiny core, of the island I lived on for a few weeks. You will say to me 'solitude'. You will remind me that I must try to be alone for part of each year, even a week or a few days; and for part of each day, even for an hour or a few minutes in order to keep my core, my centre, my island-quality. You will remind me that unless I keep the island-quality intact somewhere within me, I will have little to give my husband, my children, my friends or the world at large. You will remind me that woman must be still as the axis of a wheel in the midst of her activities; that she must be the pioneer in achieving this stillness, not only for her own salvation, but for the salvation of family life, of society, perhaps even of our civilization.

Anne Morrow Lindbergh (20th century)

OCTOBER 29

The attitude which brings about salvation is not like any form of activity. The Greek word which expresses it is *hypomene*, and *patientia* is rather an inadequate translation of it. It is the waiting or attentive and faithful immobility which lasts indefinitely and cannot be shaken. The slave, who waits near the door so as to open immediately the master knocks, is the best image of it. He must be ready to die of hunger and exhaustion rather than change his attitude. It must be possible for his companions to call him, talk to him, hit him, without his even turning his head. Even if he is told that the master is dead, and even if he believes it, he will not move. If he is told that the master is angry with him and will beat him when he returns, and if he believes it, he will not move.

Attention animated by desire is the whole foundation of religious practices.

Simone Weil (20th century)

October 30

To yield again and again to the calls God gives us, to come up higher when we are humanly convinced we have gone as high as we can go, this takes a special kind of courage. After each miracle God works in our lives, we may be grateful, but we are inclined to shut the door after it, as though one or two miracles were all one could expect, or tolerate, in one lifetime. But the Lord, more often than not, has something else in mind for us. As soon as we have caught our breath, he is asking us to start climbing again.

Emilie Griffin (20th century)

October 31

Of all Jesus' sayings, the one that most probably comes down to us close to its original form is the Lord's Prayer. Here the word 'heaven' is used as a symbol for the dwelling-place of God. But there is not the slightest notion that the kingdom means that we human beings are going to dwell in heaven. Rather, the kingdom means that the conditions of heaven will come down and reign here on earth. The kingdom, for whose coming Jesus taught people to pray, is defined quite simply as 'God's will done on earth'. God's will done on earth means the fulfilment of peoples' basic human, physical and social needs: daily bread, remission of debts, which includes both the wrongs that we have done others, and also the financial indebtedness that holds the poor in bondage to the weak, avoidance of the temptations that lead us to oppress one another, even in God's name, and finally, deliverance from evil. There is nothing to suggest that his vision includes conquest of death.

Rosemary Radford Ruether (20th century)

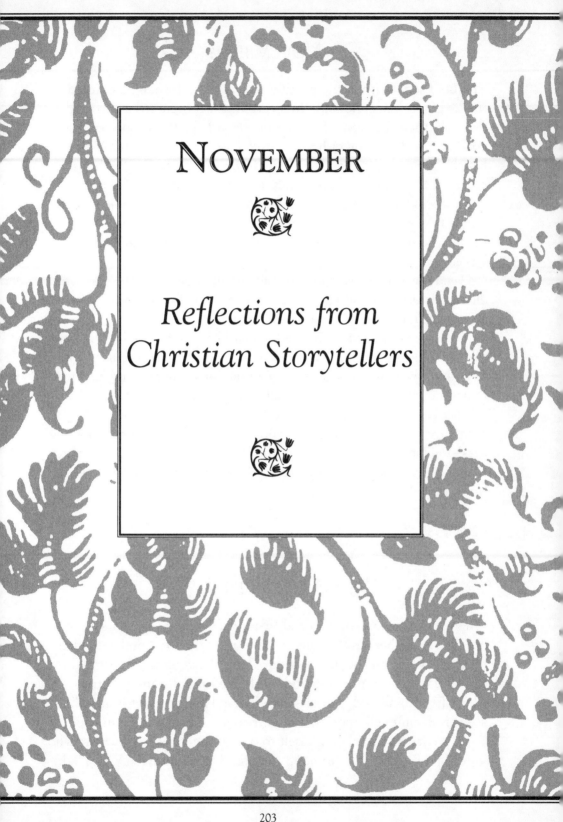

NOVEMBER

Reflections from Christian Storytellers

❧ NOVEMBER 1 ❧

The Lord sent Nathan the prophet to David, and when he entered the king's presence, he said, 'In a certain town there lived two men, one rich, the other poor. The rich man had large flocks and herds; the poor man had nothing of his own except one little ewe lamb he had bought. He reared it, and it grew up in his home together with his children. It shared his food, drank from his cup, and nestled in his arms; it was like a daughter to him. One day a traveller came to the rich man's house, and he, too mean to take something from his own flock or herd to serve to his guest, took the poor man's lamb and served that up.'

David was very angry, and burst out, 'As the Lord lives, the man who did this deserves to die! He shall pay for the lamb four times over, because he has done this and shown no pity.'

Nathan said to David, 'You are the man! This is the word of the Lord the God of Israel to you: I anointed you king over Israel, I rescued you from the power of Saul, I gave you your master's daughter and his wives to be your own. I gave you the daughters of Israel and Judah; and, had this not been enough, I would have added other favours as well. Why then have you flouted the Lord's word by doing what is wrong in my eyes? You have struck down Uriah the Hittite with the sword; the man himself you murdered by the sword of the Ammonites, and you have stolen his wife.'

2 Samuel 12:1–9

❧ NOVEMBER 2 ❧

'There was once a man who had two sons; and the younger said to his father, "Father, give me my share of the property." So he divided his estate between them. A few days later the younger son turned the whole of his share into cash and left home for a distant country, where he squandered it in dissolute living. He had spent it all, when a severe famine fell upon that country and he began to be in need. So he went and attached himself to one of the local landowners, who sent him on to his farm to mind the pigs. He would have been glad to fill his belly with the pods that the pigs were eating, but no one gave him anything. Then he came to his senses: "How many of my father's hired servants have more food than they can eat," he said, "and here am I, starving to death! I will go at once to my father, and say to him, 'Father, I have sinned against God and against you; I am no longer fit to be called your son; treat me as one of your hired servants.'" So he set out for his father's house. But while he was still a long way off his father saw him, and his heart went out to him; he ran to meet him, flung his arms round him, and kissed him. The son said, "Father, I have sinned against God and against you; I am no longer fit to be called your son." But the father said to his servants, "Quick! Fetch a robe, the best we have, and put it on him; put a ring on his finger and sandals on his feet. Bring the fatted calf and kill it, and let us celebrate with a feast. For this son of mine was dead and has come back to life; he was lost and is found." And the festivities began.

'Now the elder son had been out on the farm; and on his way back, as he approached the house, he heard music and dancing. He called one of the servants and asked what it meant. The servant told him, "Your brother has come home, and your father has killed the fatted calf because he has him back safe and sound." But he was angry and refused to go in. His father came out and pleaded with him; but he retorted, "You know how I have slaved for you all these years; I never once disobeyed your orders; yet you never gave me so much as a kid, to celebrate with my friends. But now that this son of yours turns up, after running through your money with his women, you kill the fatted calf for him." "My boy," said the father, "you are always with me, and everything I have is yours. How could we fail to celebrate this happy day? Your brother here was dead and has come back to life; he was lost and has been found."'

Luke 15:11–32

🏵 NOVEMBER 3 🏵

'A man was on his way from Jerusalem down to Jericho when he was set upon by robbers, who stripped and beat him, and went off leaving him half dead. It so happened that a priest was going down by the same road, and when he saw him, he went past on the other side. So too a Levite came to the place, and when he saw him went past on the other side. But a Samaritan who was going that way came upon him, and when he saw him he was moved to pity. He went up and bandaged his wounds, bathing them with oil and wine. Then he lifted him on to his own beast, brought him to an inn, and looked after him. Next day he produced two silver pieces and gave them to the innkeeper, and said, "Look after him; and if you spend more, I will repay you on my way back."

'Which of these three do you think was neighbour to the man who fell into the hands of the robbers?' He answered, 'The one who showed him kindness.' Jesus said to him, 'Go and do as he did.'

Luke 10:30–37

🌸 NOVEMBER 4 🌸

One night a man had a dream. He dreamed he was walking along the beach with the Lord. Across the sky flashed scenes from his life. For each scene, he noticed two sets of footprints in the sand: one belonging to him, and the other to the Lord.

When the last scene of his life flashed before him, he looked back at the footprints in the sand. He noticed that many times along the path of his life there was only one set of footprints. He also noticed that it happened at the very lowest and saddest times in his life.

This really bothered him and he questioned the Lord about it. 'Lord, you said that once I decided to follow you, you would walk with me all the way. But I have noticed that during the most troublesome times of my life, there is only one set of footprints. I don't understand why, when I needed you most, you would leave me.'

The Lord replied, 'I love you and would never leave you. During your times of trial and suffering, when you see only one set of footprints, it was then that I carried you.'

Margaret Fishback Powers (20th century), from Footprints

A wise old woman was once asked what God is like. In reply she told a story, of five blind men who set out to discover what an elephant was like.

They eventually were taken to one, and felt it all over. One found the trunk and announced: 'It's like a snake!'

Another found its tail and said that, to his way of thinking, 'it's more like a rope!'

A third touched one of the animal's ears, and became convinced that an elephant was like a fan.

'No, it's not, it's like a pillar!' said the fourth, feeling a great leg.

While the last man rested against the side of the beast, and declared that an elephant was certainly most like a huge wall.

Anonymous

Saint Jerome lived with his friends in a large house set amongst fields, in the middle of a large forest. Every day the friends would rise early and, after breakfast, set out for a day's work in the fields, or a day's wood-chopping in the forest.

One day, everybody had gone off to work from the house except Jerome. Halfway through the morning, he was interrupted by the frightened cries of men running for safety from their work in the woods. When he went to find out the cause of their flight he was told that they had been surprised by a large and very fierce-looking lion. Not long afterwards, those who had been busy in the fields also fled home, for they too had been terrified by the sudden appearance of a ferocious lion, roaring loudly.

And then, while all of them were sitting down to lunch, there came the sound of this same lion, making the most terrifying noises, from just outside the front door. Everyone was frightened out of their wits, except Jerome. 'I'll go and see what's the matter with brother lion,' he said, and made for the door, despite the anxious pleas of his friends.

Opening the door, he stepped outside. There, was quite the biggest lion he had ever seen, roaring loudly. 'Now what is the matter with you, brother lion?' asked Jerome. The animal sat on its back haunches and lifted up one of its front paws. Embedded in the paw was a rusty nail. Jerome called for some warm water and a bandage, and then as carefully as he could he extracted the nail from the lion's paw. 'He means no harm,' he called to his friends, 'he just needs some help.'

Anonymous

🌸 NOVEMBER 7 🌸

Once upon a time seven old men decided to dedicate their lives to the service of God. They went to live in a forest, where they held services several times a day.

None of the old men could sing, so they said their services. But the evening service contained a hymn of which they were all very fond, and they were determined that they would sing that if nothing else. So every evening their worship would end with the seven of them singing lustily. None of them sang in tune, and each had a different idea of what the tune should be, so it was not a good sound! Even the birds in the forest would put their wings over their ears rather than endure it.

One Christmas Eve, a passing traveller joined them for evening worship. They were very pleased to have him join them, especially when he told them that he was a professional singer. 'Now we shall be able to sing our hymn properly,' they thought. Indeed, the visitor sung so well, that the old men fell silent in admiration, and let him sing the hymn by himself.

What the old men did not know was that their guest was a rather conceited fellow, who took great pride in the quality of his voice. As a result his song never reached heaven. At the end of the service, after their visitor had retired to bed, the seven old men were visited by an angel, 'Why has no sweet music been offered in praise of God on this of all nights?' enquired the angel.

Then the seven old men realized that their singing, poor as it might be, was acceptable to God, and so they went back to the church and sang their hymn again, this time by themselves!

Anonymous

The ruler of a certain kingdom taught his people that if they lived good lives, then they would be happy after death, but if they didn't, they would be miserable. He believed this deeply, but was never quite sure why!

One night he had a dream. He dreamed that he had died and was being taken by an angel to a place of happiness. But he was worried about the fate of those of his people who had died and were now miserable. So, he asked if he could go and see them.

'Certainly,' said the angel, and they took him to a beautiful land, where the sun was shining, the sky was blue and the buildings were magnificent. He was taken into a hall, full of tables laden with every sort of food. 'There must be a mistake,' said the king, 'nobody could possibly be unhappy here.' 'Ah' said the angel, 'you see there is a rule in this place: the food must be eaten using chopsticks six-foot long.' Then the king understood the pain of those who lived there.

'Come along,' said the angel, 'this is not the place for you.' The king was then taken to the place of happiness. There, too, the sky was blue, the sun was shining, and the countryside was beautiful. He was led into a hall full of tables laden with every sort of food. 'But this is just the same as the other place, only here the people look happy,' he said, 'except, I suppose, they don't have that rule about the chopsticks being six-foot long?'

'Yes, they do,' said the angel, 'they have to use those chopsticks here too.'

'Then how is it that the people are so happy?' said the king.

'In this place,' answered the angel, 'they've learnt to feed each other.'

Anonymous

A long time ago there lived a poor man, who discovered quite by chance, that he had a gift for juggling – such a gift that he was able to make a respectable living from it. However, he eventually grew tired of juggling, feeling that there must be something more worthwhile that he could do with his life. For a time he went to live in a monastery. He gave the monks what money he had, and they allowed him to stay, and set him some humble tasks to do about the community. For a while he was happy, glad not still to be juggling; but as time passed he grew increasingly frustrated with his life, finding little point in any of it.

In desperation, he dragged himself into the monastery church, and finding a statue of the Virgin Mary, threw himself down in front of it. There he poured out his pain to the wooden figure. Eventually, exhausted, he just lay there on the stone floor.

As he lay there, he heard a quiet voice speaking to him, 'Give what you have,' it seemed to say. 'But I have nothing to give,' he moaned. The voice spoke again, 'Give what you have.'

Slowly, he got to his feet. Finding some candles in front of the statue, he began to juggle with them, faster and faster, better and better: juggling for the Virgin Mary. When the abbot and the other monks came looking for him, they found him there in the chapel, giving all that he had to give.

Anonymous

🌸 NOVEMBER 10 🌸

A woman was once walking in the mountains. She was following a narrow path, up and up. Turning a corner in the path, she saw a mountain goat going up the same path some way ahead of her. Climbing onwards, she then saw a second goat coming down the path in the opposite direction.

Soon the two goats would meet, and the path was too narrow for them to pass each other. 'I wonder what they'll do?' she thought, 'perhaps there will be a fight, and the weaker goat will be knocked over the edge of the path and killed.' She wished she could do something to prevent the imminent disaster, but she was helpless.

But when the two goats met each other, they knew just what to do. Without as much as a pause, the goat that was climbing up the path lay down, and the goat that was coming down stepped over it. Then they both went quietly on their way.

Anonymous

Just before the First World War, Jean Giono was walking through a
mountain region of France. The countryside was desolate, with
abandoned villages and dried up water courses. Nothing grew on the
barren soil.

He ran out of water and became desperately thirsty. Struggling on, he
saw, in the distance, a small figure. When he reached it, he found it was
a shepherd with some sheep. He gave Jean some of his water, and later
took him back to his stone house for the night. After they had eaten,
the shepherd asked him to help sort through a bag of acorns.

The next morning they went walking together. The shepherd carried
an iron rod. And when they came to the top of a ridge, he began making
holes in the ground and dropping the acorns into them. He told how he
had already planted over ten thousand, and hoped to plant many more.
He felt the countryside was dying for lack of trees, and he hoped to
bring it alive again. He also had a little nursery of beech seedlings, which
he intended to transplant when they were big enough.

Mr Giono left his kind host, and never saw him again. But years later
he returned to the same mountain region and found it transformed. The
oak trees were now a small forest, and there were beeches as high as his
shoulder. More amazingly, the water had returned, and was running in
streams. Reeds and rushes were growing on the banks, flowers and
grasses on the earth. People had repopulated the villages, rebuilding the
houses and replanting the gardens.

Author's retelling

Once there was a man who had grown weary of life. Tired to death.
So one day he decided to leave his home town, his ancestral village,
to search for the perfect Magical City where all would be different,
new, full and rewarding. So he left. On his journey he found himself in
a forest. So he settled down for the night, took out his sack and had a
bite to eat. Before he turned in for sleep he was careful to take off his
shoes and point them to the new direction towards which he was going.

However, unknown to him, while he slept a jokester came during the night and turned his shoes around. When the man awoke the next morning he carefully stepped into his shoes and continued on to the Magical City.

After a few days, he came to the Magical City. Not quite as large as he had imagined it, however. In fact, it looked somewhat familiar. He found a familiar street, knocked at a familiar door, met a familiar family he found there and lived happily ever after.

William Bausch (20th century)

🌼 NOVEMBER 13 🌼

Once upon a time there was an old man from the lovely island of Crete. He loved his land with a deep and beautiful intensity, so much that when he perceived that he was about to die he had his sons bring him outside and lay him on his beloved earth. As he was about to expire he reached down by his side and clutched some earth into his hands. He died a happy man.

He now appeared before Heaven's gates. God, as an old white-bearded man, came out to greet him. 'Welcome,' he said. 'You've been a good man. Please, come into the joys of heaven.' But as the old man started to enter the pearly gates, God said, 'Please. You must let the soil go.' 'Never!' said the old man stepping back. 'Never!' And so God departed sadly, leaving the old man outside the gates. A few eons went by. God came out again, this time as a friend, an old drinking crony. They had a few drinks, told some stories, and then God said, 'All right, now it's time to enter heaven, friend. Let's go.' And they started for the pearly gates. And once more God requested that the old man let go of his soil and once more he refused.

More eons rolled by. God came out once more, this time as a delightful and playful granddaughter. 'Oh, Granddaddy,' she said, 'you're so wonderful and we all miss you. Please come inside with me.' The old man nodded and she helped him up, for by this time he had grown very old and arthritic. In fact, so arthritic was he that he had to prop up the right hand holding Crete's soil with his left hand. They moved towards the pearly gates and at this point his strength quite gave out. His gnarled fingers would no longer stay clenched in a fist with the result that the soil sifted out between them until his hand was empty. He then entered heaven. The first thing he saw was his beloved island.

William Bausch (20th century)

🌸 NOVEMBER 14 🌸

Beyond the movements of [three men at a busy airport] stands the dark figure of the bishop. They are men in their forties, like him. Nothing very special about them, except that they are dressed as some gay men do. From their talking two are English and one American. The American does not look very well. Thin and grey in the face, his leather jacket hanging loose from his shoulders… The three are saying goodbye. They are standing close together, arms about each other in an embrace and a hug. From time to time one will kiss the other and pat his back. One of them brushes away tears with the back of his hand, suddenly laughing at his own emotions, a little embarrassed perhaps…

A discreet man, [the bishop] does not want to stare too pointedly. His eyes slide towards the three, then quickly look away. His fingers tighten round the beads as he jerks them a little quicker. He does not like what he has seen. Then his eyes are back again, suspicious, and he catches a trinitarian hug. He frowns disapproval, shaking his head. He turns away in a scowl of disgust, of terror, but in his own mind he cannot leave them alone… For me the bishop and the three friends are pictures of how we envision God. Two manifestations of divinity. The bishop's God is somewhere over the rainbow, way up high. He is distant, unapproachable, unengaged in human affairs except as the God of controlling power, looking down on us, watching us, watching our mistakes… With this God there is no satisfaction and no delight, but always disapproval…

The three friends signal that love, not hatred, is the heart of God. In their support and care of one another they say to me: God is our friend and not our enemy. In their touch and in their mutuality they say that God is with us. God is by us.

Mark Pryce (20th century)

❦ NOVEMBER 15 ❦

I remembered one morning when I discovered a cocoon in the bark of a tree, just as the butterfly was making a hole in its case and preparing to come out. I waited a while, but it was too long appearing and I was impatient. I bent over it and breathed on it to warm it. I warmed it as quickly as I could and the miracle began to happen before my eyes, faster than life. The case opened, the butterfly started slowly crawling out and I shall never forget my horror when I saw how its wings were folded back and crumpled; the wretched butterfly tried with its whole trembling body to unfold them. Bending over it, I tried to help it with my breath. In vain. It needed to be hatched out patiently and the unfolding of the wings should be a gradual process in the sun. Now it was too late. My breath had forced the butterfly to appear, all crumpled, before its time. It struggled desperately and, a few seconds later, died in the palm of my hand.

That little body is, I do believe, the greatest weight I have on my conscience. For I realize today that it is a mortal sin to violate the great laws of nature. We should not hurry, we should not be impatient, but we should confidently obey the eternal rhythm.

Nikos Kazantzakis (1883–1957)

❦ NOVEMBER 16 ❦

The wise man was out doing his gardening one day, when people began rushing past his house in a great hurry. Stopping one of the crowd, he asked where they were going in such haste. 'Haven't you heard? The king is giving a party and everyone is invited.'

Quickly the man hurried after the crowd to the king's palace. He was late getting there. When the master of ceremonies saw him in his gardening clothes he was shown to the very bottom of the hall, well out of sight of the king. It would be hours before he was served! So he got up and went home.

He now dressed himself in his finest clothes, and returned to the party looking like a lord. Taking him for a man of some importance, the master of ceremonies showed him to the king's table, where a large dish of wonderful food was placed before him.

Without a pause, the wise man started scooping up the food with his hands, and smearing it all over his magnificent clothes. The king was somewhat taken aback. 'Your Eminence,' he said, 'I am curious as to your eating habits, which are rather new to me!'

'Nothing special,' said the wise man, 'but the clothes got me in here and procured my food for me, so surely they deserve their share?'

Anonymous

NOVEMBER 17

A group of Christians had met together to pray. They talked about what they were to do, and inevitably they disagreed amongst themselves. So they decided, each of them in their own way, to pray for guidance. When they had finished, one of the members said that he felt sure that his prayer had been answered: Jesus would be with them next time they met and would show them what to do. Some were sceptical about this but none had the courage to oppose the idea.

Sure enough when they met a week later, suddenly there was Jesus in their midst. 'I expect you all know the prayer I taught my disciples?' he asked. They all nodded. 'And you believe and trust in the Holy Spirit?' he asked. Again they all nodded. 'Then there's nothing for me to add,' said Jesus and disappeared.

They were mystified by all this, and the bright spark whose idea this had been was asked to pray again. He did so. 'Jesus will join us again next week,' he announced.

A week later Jesus was again in their midst. 'I expect you all know the prayer I taught my disciples? he asked. They all shook their heads. 'And you believe and trust in the Holy Spirit? he asked. Again they shook their heads. 'Well, you're too ignorant for me to waste my time on,' said Jesus and disappeared.

By now they were really quite irritated with the one who's idea this had all been. He was asked to pray for a third time, and when he told them that Jesus would be coming again the next week they laid their plans.

Sure enough, a week later, there was Jesus in their midst. 'I expect you all know the prayer I taught my disciples? he asked. Forewarned, half the group nodded while the other half shook their heads. 'Do you believe and trust in the Holy Spirit? he asked. Again, half nodded and half shook their heads. 'Well,' said Jesus, 'those of you who do know and believe had better help those of you who don't.' And he disappeared.

Anonymous

✿ NOVEMBER 18 ✿

One day in the middle of autumn, I left my house to go for a walk. I was feeling depressed, and needed a change of scene. Moodily I was kicking through the leaves on the grass opposite my home, when I noticed a small boy coming towards me. 'Hallo Henry,' he said, 'would you like some crisps?' and he offered me an open bag of salt and vinegar crisps. Now I don't much care for salt and vinegar flavour crisps, but it seemed churlish to quibble, so I thanked him, and helped myself to a handful. Munching them, I continued on my way. Suddenly I realized that my sense of depression had gone. I had been visited by an angel! I had received a act of love. And I felt a new man.

Henry Morgan (20th century)

✿ NOVEMBER 19 ✿

A passenger tells how he was once invited into the cockpit of a Boeing 747 bound for Hawaii, from Los Angeles. There he saw a little black box. 'This is a computer,' he was told. 'Every time the plane goes off course this computer (which does the navigation) tells another computer how many degrees off course the plane is, and the other computer (which does the steering) makes the necessary adjustment to keep the plane flying in the right direction.' The 747 is technically 'off course' for about ninety per cent of the time during its flight to Hawaii. But every few seconds a correction is made by the computers acting together. The plane has never failed to reach Hawaii.

We get to our destination not by going straight there, but by learning to make the necessary adjustments on the way.

Anonymous

NOVEMBER 20

An elderly woman who was an enthusiastic gardener declared that she had no faith whatsoever in predictions that some scientists would learn to control the weather. According to her, all that was needed to control the weather was prayer.

Then, one summer, while she was away on a foreign trip, a drought hit the land and wiped out her entire garden. She was so upset when she got back that she changed her religion.

Anthony de Mello (20th century)

NOVEMBER 21

Of a saint it used to be said that each time he left home to go and perform his religious duties he would say, 'And now, Lord, goodbye! I am off to church.'

Anthony de Mello (20th century)

NOVEMBER 22

Once the Master was at prayer. The disciples came up to him and said, 'Sir, teach us how to pray.' This is what he taught them...

Two men were once walking through a field when they saw an angry bull. Instantly they made for the nearest fence with the bull in hot pursuit. It soon became evident to them that they were not going to make it, so one man said to the other, 'We've had it! Nothing can save us. Say a prayer. Quick!'

The other shouted back, 'I've never prayed in my life and I don't have a prayer for this occasion.'

'Never mind. The bull is catching up with us. Any prayer will do.'

'Well, I'll say the one I remember my father used to say before meals: For what we are about to receive, Lord, make us truly grateful.'

Anthony de Mello (20th century)

NOVEMBER 23

An old man would sit motionless for hours on end in church. One day a priest asked him what God talked to him about.

'God doesn't talk. He just listens,' was his reply.

'Well, then what do you talk to him about?'

'I don't talk either. I just listen.'

Anthony de Mello (20th century)

NOVEMBER 24

An efficiency expert was making his report to Henry Ford. 'As you will see, sir, the report is highly favourable, except for that man down the hall. Every time I pass by he's sitting with his feet on his desk. He's wasting your money.'

Said Ford, 'That man once had an idea that earned us a fortune. At the time I believe his feet were exactly where they are now.'

Anthony de Mello (20th century)

NOVEMBER 25

An atheist fell off a cliff. As he tumbled downward he caught hold of a branch of a small tree. There he hung a thousand feet above the rocks below.

Then he had an idea. 'God!' he shouted with all his might.

Silence!

'God!' he shouted again.

Then he heard a loud Voice, 'Let go, and I'll catch you.'

'Let go!' said the man, 'Do you think I'm crazy?'

Anthony de Mello (20th century)

NOVEMBER 26

A Hindu Sage was having the Life of Jesus read to him.

When he learned how Jesus was rejected by his people in Nazareth, he exclaimed, 'A rabbi whose congregation does not want to drive him out of town isn't a rabbi.'

And when he heard how it was the priests who put Jesus to death, he said with a sigh, 'It is hard for Satan to mislead the whole world, so he appoints prominent ecclesiastics in different parts of the globe.'

Anthony de Mello (20th century)

NOVEMBER 27

Said a preacher to a friend, 'We have just had the greatest revival our church has experienced in many years.'

'How many did you add to your church membership?'

'None. We lost five hundred.'

Anthony de Mello (20th century)

NOVEMBER 28

There was an old farmer who had an old horse for tilling his fields. One day the horse escaped into the hills, and when the old farmer's neighbours sympathized with the old man over his bad luck, the farmer replied, 'Bad luck? Good luck? Who knows?' A week later the horse returned with a herd of wild horses from the hills and this time the neighbours congratulated the farmer on his good luck. His reply was, 'Good luck? Bad luck? Who knows?' Then, when the farmer's son was attempting to tame one of the wild horses, he fell off its back and broke his leg. Everyone thought this was very bad luck. Not the farmer, whose only reaction was, 'Bad luck? Good luck? Who knows?' Some weeks later the army marched into the village and conscripted every able-bodied youth they found there. When they saw the farmer's son with his broken leg they let him off. Now was that good luck? Bad luck? Who knows? Everything that seems on the surface to be evil may be a good in disguise. And everything that seems good on the surface may really be an evil. So we are wise when we leave it to God to decide what is good luck and what bad, and thank him that all things turn out for good with those who love him.

Anthony de Mello (20th century)

❧ NOVEMBER 29 ❧

A monk in his travels once found a precious stone and kept it. One day he met a traveller, and when the monk opened his bag to share his provisions with him, the traveller saw the jewel and asked the monk to give it to him. The monk did so readily. The traveller departed, overjoyed with the unexpected gift of the precious stone that was enough to give him wealth and security for the rest of his life. However, a few days later he came back in search of the monk, found him, gave him back the stone, and entreated him, 'Now give me something much more precious than this stone, valuable as it is. Give me that which enabled you to give it to me.'

Anthony de Mello (20th century)

❧ NOVEMBER 30 ❧

A Christian monk who escaped persecution by fleeing over some mountains at considerable risk to his own life, was asked how on earth he had managed such a perilous journey alone. He replied: 'One step at a time.'

Author's retelling

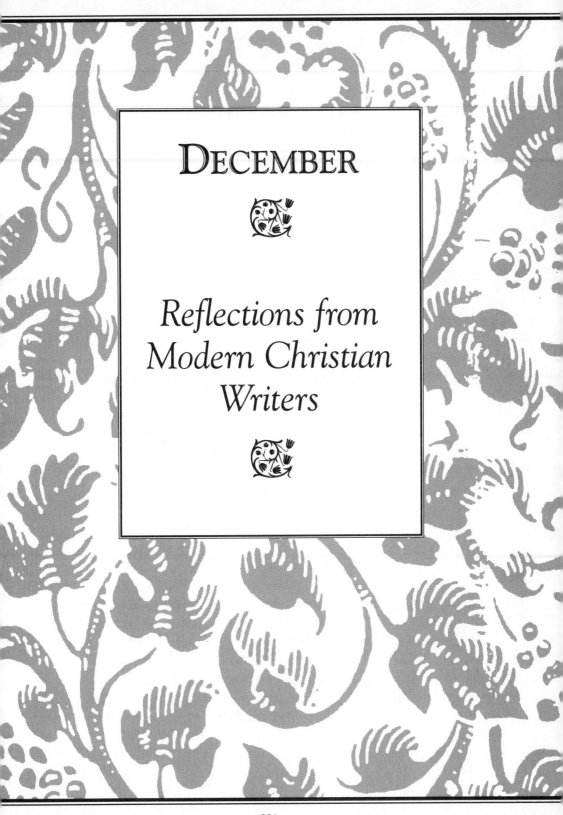

DECEMBER

*Reflections from
Modern Christian
Writers*

❦ DECEMBER 1 ❦

In the great tradition of Christian prayer, true prayer is the naked
standing before God as a creature before our Creator and as a penitent
before our Saviour. This brings with it a growing awareness of the
majesty of God and a growing realization of our utter nothingness before
him. That is why all the great Saints have genuinely believed themselves
to be the greatest of sinners.

Mother Mary Clare

❦ DECEMBER 2 ❦

The imagery of popular devotion suggests a divine supremacy over the
universe. Supremacy is not the relationship of the artist to the work of
art, nor of the lover to the object of his love. That God should be
superior, in every or any respect, to an inferior universe is a quite
illegitimate deduction from the doctrine of creation. If the work of God
in creation is the work of love, then truth demands an imagery which
will do justice to the limitless self-giving which is among the marks of
authentic love.

As a parenthesis, we may illustrate the kind of imagery which might
express the self-giving of God in creation. A doctor tells of an operation
which, as a young student, he observed in a London hospital. 'It was the
first time that this particular brain operation had been carried out in this
country. It was performed by one of our leading surgeons upon a young
man of great promise for whom, after an accident, there seemed to be
no other remedy. It was an operation of the greatest delicacy, in which a
small error would have had fatal consequences. In the outcome the
operation was a triumph: but it involved seven hours of intense and
uninterrupted concentration on the part of the surgeon. When it was
over, a nurse had to take him by the hand, and lead him from the
operating theatre like a blind man or a little child.' This, one might say,
is what self-giving is like: such is the likeness of God, wholly given, spent
and drained in that sublime self-giving which is the ground and source
and origin of the universe.

W.H. Vanstone

❧ DECEMBER 3 ❧

Walking in the street I feel rising from time an inscrutable sadness, from out of the stones a patience. What is this far calling longing? What are these flowing echoes? The beautiful hard skin of trees springing up into the sky, my father's hand parts the leaves at the end of the wood; in the cool length of the evening it is a voice speaking in the mystery sorrow of the sinking fire of the sun, the day is mournful and wishes to cleanse itself in darkness. It is now as a child I feel the mystical sexual life of the elements, the hard stones and yielding plants, the lashing of water upon them, how they lift up their heads to consume the sunlight, how they live in the light of the rising moon with a stillness, with holy sex nerves drinking the subtle light of planetary love.

It is this hidden under flowing of girls and women who carry this mystical sexuality – that draws me into the trance of nature, healing me, for natural love can heal us; this natural poetical love of nature can bring us happiness, but many things interrupt such a love; mean ambitions, worldly desire to appear above and to dominate others, fame, lastly the Spirit; our problem is how [to] bring corruption into harmony, into relation with eternal Spirit; the basis of our life is war between the eternal corruption of nature and the Spirit.

Cecil Collins

❧ DECEMBER 4 ❧

Forgiveness is understanding and holding the pain of another;
    it is compassion.
Forgiveness is the acceptance of our brokenness, yours and mine.
Forgiveness is letting go of unrealistic expectations of others.
    and of the desire that they be other than they are.
Forgiveness is liberating others to be themselves, not making them feel
    guilty for what may have been…
Forgiveness is peace-making:
    struggling to create unity,
    to build one body,
    to heal the broken body of humanity.

Jean Vanier, 'Forgiveness in Community'

DECEMBER 5

In the early sixteenth century, the artist Grunewald painted an altarpiece depicting the crucifixion. The torn, lacerated body of Christ is also covered in hundreds of sores, sores that obviously add to the agony of the dying Christ. In those days central Europe was wracked by a disease that caused those around to recoil with fear. The sores on the body of Grunewald's Christ were the syphilitic sores of Christ's suffering humanity. The symbolism is clear: the body of Christ, the Church, suffered from the scourges of the world, and at that moment the scourge was a sexually transmitted deadly disease for which, in that moment of time, there was no cure.

Today, some four hundred and fifty years later, the body of Christ is suffering. The body of Christ is suffering because the people of God are suffering. And once again the suffering is from disease and fear. The disease is AIDS and HIV, and the fear is just as irrational now as it was in the sixteenth century. We are all vulnerable, for we have the power to lift up those who are burdened. It is we who are called to embrace, to hold, enfold, to kiss as sisters and brothers in Christ, the thousands of women, men and children, who bear in their bodies this further mark of our fallenness. We are the body of Christ, seeking to be a community of comfort and support, and a Church of help and hope.

Anonymous

DECEMBER 6

When you travel, you experience, in a very practical way, the act of rebirth. You confront completely new situations, the day passes more slowly, and on most journeys you don't even understand the language the people speak. So you are like a child just out of the womb. You begin to attach much more importance to the things around you because your survival depends upon them. You begin to be more accessible to others because they may be able to help you in difficult situations. And you accept any small favour from the gods with great delight, as if it were an episode you would remember for the rest of your life.

At the same time, since all things are new, you see only the beauty in them, and you feel happy to be alive. That's why a religious pilgrimage has always been one of the most objective ways of achieving insight. The word peccadillo, which means a 'small sin', comes from *pecus*, which means 'defective foot', a foot that is incapable of walking a road. The way to correct the peccadillo is always to walk forward, adapting oneself to new situations and receiving in return all of the thousands of blessings that life generously offers to those who seek them.

Paulo Coelho

 DECEMBER 7

All our yesterdays and their memories
Fail to tether the undaunted spirit
That probes the future, seeking crevices,
Ever grasping for foot-holds, finger-holds,
Ready to reach beyond mundane routine.
Now is the time – the opportunity!
Only ghostly shadows flit across the
Overcast sky, but have no power to dull
Nor quench the new all-pressing impulse to
Search for ways to ease the pain that always
Holds in vice-like grip the victims of high
Int'rest rates, compounding debt, poverty
For billions unaware that they will pay
The price the rich demand, and have no say.

*John Payne Cook, 'A Sonnet for the Millennium on the Call for
Debt-relief for the Poorest Nations of the World'*

DECEMBER 8

Above all, trust in the slow work of God.
We are, quite naturally,
impatient in everything to reach the end
without delay.

We should like to skip
the intermediate stages.
We are impatient of being
on the way to something unknown,
something new,
And yet it is the law of all progress
that it is made by passing through
some stages of instability –
And that it may take a very long time.

And so I think it is with you.
Your ideas mature gradually –
let them grow,
let them shape themselves,
without undue haste.
Don't try to force them on,
as though you could be today
what time (that is to say, grace and
circumstances acting
on your own good will)
will make you tomorrow.

Only God could say what this new spirit
gradually forming within you will be.
Give our Lord the benefit of believing
that his hand is leading you,
and accept the anxiety of
feeling yourself in suspense and incomplete.

Pierre Teilhard de Chardin

🦎 DECEMBER 9 🦎

Our deepest fear is not that we are inadequate.
Our deepest fear is that we are powerful beyond measure.
It is our light, not our darkness, that most frightens us.
We ask ourselves who am I to be brilliant, gorgeous, talented and fabulous?
Actually, who are you not to be?

You are a child of God.
Your playing small doesn't serve the world.
There's nothing enlightened about shrinking so that other people won't
feel insecure around you.
We were born to make manifest the glory of God that is within us.
It's not in just some of us; it's in everyone.
And as we let our own light shine, we unconsciously give other people
permission to do the same.
As we are liberated from our own fear our presence automatically
liberates others.

Nelson Mandela quoting Marianne Williamson in his Inaugural Speech, 1994

DECEMBER 10

One day you finally knew
what you had to do, and began,
though the voices around you
kept shouting
their bad advice –
though the whole house
began to tremble
and you felt the old tug
at your ankles.
'Mend my life!'
each voice cried.
But you didn't stop.
You knew what you had to do,
though the wind pried
with its stiff fingers
at the very foundations –
though their melancholy
was terrible.
It was already late
enough, and a wild night,
and the road full of fallen
branches and stones.

But, little by little,
as you left their voices behind,
the stars began to burn
through the sheets of clouds,
and there was a new voice,
which you slowly
recognized as your own,
that kept you company
as you strode deeper and deeper
into the world,
determined to do
the only thing you could do –
determined to save
the only life you could save.

Mary Oliver, 'The Journey'

DECEMBER 11

There is something of the poet in all of us, of course, or of the painter or
the musician or the dancer or the architect. But of all the arts the living
of a life is perhaps the greatest; to live every moment of life with the
same imaginative commitment as the poet brings to a special field. The
fashion in a society whose values are material and which sets little store
on any other asks not what we 'are' but what we 'do'; worse, the phrase
'What is he worth?' has come to mean, 'How much money has he?' How
sad, how false, and what a betrayal! What we are 'worth' is not what we
have, not even what we have made or done, but what we are. Poetry is
not an end in itself but in the service of life; of what use are poems, or
any other works of art, unless to enable human lives to be lived with
insight of a deeper kind, with more sensitive feelings, more intense sense
of the beautiful, with deeper understanding? According to Plato the soul
knows everything, but in this world has forgotten; and the poem reminds
us of what we ourselves know, but did not know we knew; reminds us,
above all, of what we are.

Kathleen Raine

❦ DECEMBER 12 ❦

You are so young; you stand before beginnings. I would like to beg of you, dear friend, as well as I can, to have patience with everything that remains unsolved in your heart. Try to love the questions themselves, like locked rooms and like books written in a foreign language. Do not now look for the answers. They cannot now be given to you because you could not live with them. It is a question of experiencing everything. At present you need to live the question. Perhaps you will gradually, without even noticing it, find yourself experiencing the answer, some distant day. Perhaps you are indeed carrying within yourself the potential to visualise, to design, and to create for yourself an utterly satisfying, joyful, and pure lifestyle. Discipline yourself to attain it, but accept that which comes to you with deep trust, and as long as it comes from your own will, from your own inner need, accept it, and do not hate anything.

Rainer Maria Rilke

❦ DECEMBER 13 ❦

There are no traps or snares set for us, and there is nothing that should frighten or torture us. We are placed into life, into the element best suited to it. Beside, through thousands of years of adaptation, we have acquired such a resemblance to this life, that we, if we stood still, would hardly be distinguishable from our surroundings. We have no reason to mistrust our world, for it is not against us. If it has terrors, they are our own terrors. If it has precipices, they belong to us. If dangers are present, we must try to love them. And if we fashion our life according to that principle, which advises us to embrace that which is difficult, then that which appears to us to be the very strangest will become the most worthy of our trust, and the truest.

How could we be capable of forgetting the old myths that stand at the threshold of all mankind, myths of dragons transforming themselves at the very last moment into princesses? Perhaps all dragons in our lives are really princesses just waiting to see us just once being beautiful and courageous. Perhaps everything fearful is basically helplessness that seeks our help.

Rainer Maria Rilke

Prayer is a listening to the creative, life-giving word that loves us into being. Yet prayer of a simple, contemplative kind, in which we try to stand before God and let him know us, not much preoccupied with particular thoughts but just loving, invariably produces a sense of our own sinfulness. There seem to be two distinct kinds of sin. One is a deliberate 'No' to God in any area whatever; this automatically cancels the simple kind of prayer, until it is repented of and a 'Yes' substituted. It is obvious why this must be so: life and prayer cannot be compartmentalized. The other kind of sinfulness makes itself felt in a global sense of being weak and shabby and in need of God's mercy, an awareness of the general slum-situation within. This kind is not an act but a state, and it almost seems to help; or at least the experience of it is part of prayer. You know that you are an undeserving beggar, that you have not a leg to stand on; yet somehow it is good to be there, because it is real, and to avoid this confrontation would be to escape into untruth. The strange thing is that, although prayer is often completely unsatisfying and very humbling, although you seem to fail and fail again in prayer, you dimly know that it is all-important to stay there in that emptiness, refusing to fill the void with anything that is not God.

Maria Boulding

I look at this food I know to be the same as it always has been. But wait. My eyes are almost burned by what I see. There's a bowl in front of me that wasn't there before. A brown button bowl and in it some apricots, some small oranges, some nuts, cherries, a banana. The fruits, the colours, mesmerize me in a quiet rapture that spins through my head. I am entranced by colour. I lift an orange into the flat filthy palm of my hand and feel and smell and lick it. The colour orange, the colour, the colour, my God the colour orange. Before me is a feast of colour. I feel myself begin to dance, slowly, I am intoxicated by colour. I feel the colour in a quiet somnambulant rage. Such wonder, such absolute wonder in such an insignificant fruit.

I cannot, I will not eat this fruit. I sit in quiet joy, so complete, beyond the meaning of joy. My soul finds its own completeness in that bowl of colour. The forms of each fruit. The shape and curl and bend all so rich, so perfect. I want to bow before it, loving that blazing, roaring, orange colour… Everything meeting in a moment of colour and of form, my rapture no longer an abstract euphoria. It is there in that tiny bowl, the world recreated in that broken bowl. I feel the smell of each fruit leaping into me and lifting me and carrying me away. I am drunk with something that I understand but cannot explain. I am filled with a sense of love. I am filled and satiated by it. What I have waited and longed for has without my knowing come to me, and taken all of me.

Brian Keenan

❧ DECEMBER 16 ❧

I think that wifehood and motherhood lived consciously can be a very powerful spiritual practice in which we have an opportunity to grow every moment of the day. If a woman moves through her daily life as a wife and mother consciously letting go of her own needs, releasing anger and suffering and resentment, she's building a spirituality in herself that would probably outdistance any sacrifice the men make. But I'm only realizing this today. When I was a housewife and mother I was too bogged down to get it. I think the path of a homemaker is one that needs to be explored and offers enormous opportunities for coming to consciousness. But I never found it for myself.

Esse Chasin

❧ DECEMBER 17 ❧

For full enjoyment of sex, for true completeness, one does the same thing one does with God. One says, 'I am thine' to that force of energy that has created us. It's only when you can give over the concern about everything else – whether the bills are paid or the phone is ringing – and join that moment, join the other body, that you can have total completeness in sex. So it is the same as the development of true spirituality. You must admit to yourself that you are a part of everything, and then there is total enjoyment. In eating, in sex, in laughter, in crying – complete enjoyment, a complete joining and joy with the other. And why shouldn't we enjoy it? It's all God's gift.

Maya Angelou

DECEMBER 18

In living the youness of you,
be prepared to go outside the gate in giving all.
But first, keep asking,
What is your deepest desire now?
In desiring to give yourself utterly,
do not do so prematurely,
before you have become the fullest self
that it is possible for you to become.
There are many lesser desirings and givings
that must have their place.
Not least among these are affection, companionship,
falling asleep in the arms of those who love you,
the making of love.
And when such lesser desires are being fulfilled,
rejoice in what is, however incomplete.
If you expect all,
you will be worshipping an idol,
not enjoying life with another human being.

Jim Cotter

DECEMBER 19

Prayer! Prayer! Prayer!
May heaven accept this prayer of mine
repeated over and over again for many months.

May the edge of my soul become sharper.
Even if my breast explodes in agonized wailing,
let me set out on this journey.
Let me go out into the wilderness,
into the land that nearly drives me mad
with its awakening bitterness.
The land over which stars sparkle
in the frozen winter dawn.
Let me pray alone,
let me decide alone:
to be with the people, at the bottom,
to be beaten with them,
to decay with them,
and finally to rise up gallantly from the earth
with them
in the bright morning sunshine,
with our heads held high.

Kim Chi Ha

❧ DECEMBER 20 ❧

Lord, Holy Spirit,
You are as the mother eagle with her young,
Holding them in peace under your feathers.
On the highest mountain you have built your nest,
Above the valley, above the storms of the world,
Where no hunter ever comes.

Lord, Holy Spirit,
You are the bright cloud in whom we hide,
In whom we know already that
the battle has been won.
You bring us to our Brother Jesus
To rest our heads upon his shoulder.

Lord, Holy Spirit,
In the love of friends you are building a new house,

Heaven is with us when you are with us.
You are singing your song in the hearts of the poor.
Guide us, wound us, heal us. Bring us to God.

James K. Baxter

❧ DECEMBER 21 ❧

Hindu India developed a magnificent image to describe God's relationship with creation. God 'dances' creation. God is the dancer, creation is his dance. The dance is different from the dancer yet it has no existence apart from him. You cannot take it home in a box. The moment the dancer stops, the dance ceases to be.

In our quest for God, we think too much, reflect too much, talk too much. Even when we look at the dance we call creation, we are all the time thinking, talking (to ourselves and others), reflecting, analysing, philosophizing. Words. Noise.

Be silent and contemplate the Dance. Just look. A star, a flower, a fading leaf, a bird, a stone and fragment of the Dance will do. And hopefully, it won't be long before you see the Dancer!

Anthony de Mello

❧ DECEMBER 22 ❧

Many poets are not poets for the same reason that many religious men are not saints: they never succeed in being themselves. They never get around to being the particular poet or the particular monk they are intended to be by God. They never become the man or artist who is called for by all the circumstances or their individual lives.

They waste their years in vain efforts to be some other poet, some other saint. For many absurd reasons, they are convinced that they are obliged to become somebody else who died two hundred years ago and who lived in circumstances utterly alien to their own.

They wear out their minds and bodies in a hopeless endeavour to have somebody else's experiences or write somebody else's poems or possess somebody else's sanctity.

A Catholic poet should be an apostle by being first of all a poet, not try to be a poet by being first of all an apostle. For if he presents himself to people as a poet, he is going to be judged as a poet, and if he is not a good one his apostolate will be ridiculed.

Thomas Merton

🕮 DECEMBER 23 🕮

God leaves me free to be whatever I like.
I can be myself, or not, as I please.
I am at liberty to be real, or to be unreal.
I may be true or false, the choice is mine.
I may wear now one mask and now another,
and never, if I so desire, appear with my own true face.

To work out my own identity in God,
which the Bible calls 'working out our salvation',
is a labour that requires sacrifice and anguish, risk and many tears.

I do not know clearly beforehand what the result of this work will be,
The secret of my full identity is hidden in him.
He alone can make me who I am,
Or rather who I will be when at last I fully begin to be.

Thomas Merton

🕮 DECEMBER 24 🕮

We told our stories
That's all.
We sat and listened to
Each other
And heard the journeys
Of each soul.

We sat in silence
Entering each one's pain and
Sharing each one's joy.
We heard love's longing
And the lonely reachings-out
For love and affirmation.
We heard of dreams
Shattered
And visions fled.
Of hopes and laughter
Turned stale and dark.
We felt the pain of
Isolation and
The bitterness
Of death.

But in each brave and
Lonely story
God's gentle life
Broke through
And we heard music in
The darkness
And smelt flowers in
The void.
We felt the budding
Of creation
In the searchings of
Each soul
And discerned the beauty
Of God's hand in
Each muddy, twisted path.

And God's voice sang
In each story
God's life sprang from
Each death.
Our sharing became
One story
Of a simple lonely search

For life and hope and
Oneness
In a world which sobs
For love.
And we knew that in
Our sharing
God's voice with
Mighty breath
Was saying
Love each other and
Take each other's hand.

For you are one
Though many
And in each of you
I live
So listen to my story
And share my pain
And death.
Oh, listen to my story
And rise and live
With me.

Edwina Gateley, 'The Sharing'

❦ DECEMBER 25 ❦

The central message of the New Testament is that there is really only
one prayer and that is the prayer of Christ. It is a prayer that continues
in our hearts day and night. It is the stream of love that flows constantly
between Jesus and his Father. It is the Holy Spirit.

It is the most important task of any fully human life to become as open
as possible to this stream of love. We have to allow this prayer to become
our prayer, to enter into the experience of being swept beyond ourselves
into this wonderful prayer of Jesus, this great cosmic river of love.

In order for us to do this we must learn a most demanding discipline
that is a way of silence and stillness. It is as though we have to create a

space within ourselves that will allow the consciousness of the prayer of Jesus to envelop us in this powerful mystery.

John Main

❧ DECEMBER 26 ☙

We are used to thinking of prayer in terms of 'my prayer' or 'my praise' of God, and it requires a complete rethinking of our attitude to prayer to see it as a way through Jesus, with Jesus, and in Jesus. The first requirement is that we understand that we must pass beyond egoism, so that 'my' prayer is no longer even a possibility. We are summoned to see with the eyes of Christ and to love with the heart of Christ; to respond to this summons we must pass beyond egoism.

In practical terms this means learning to be so still and silent that we cease thinking about ourselves, and this is of critical importance. We must be open to the Father through Jesus, and in prayer we must become like the eye that can see but that cannot see itself.

The way we set out on this pilgrimage of 'othercentredness', is to recite a short phrase, a word that is today commonly called a mantra. The mantra is simply a means of turning our attention beyond ourselves, a way of unhooking us from our own thoughts and concerns.

John Main

❧ DECEMBER 27 ☙

In meditative prayer we are growing into what Thomas à Kempis called 'a familiar friendship with Jesus'. We are sinking down into the light and life of Christ and becoming comfortable in that posture. The perpetual presence of the Lord (omnipresence, as we say) moves from a theological dogma into a radiant reality. 'He walks with me and he talks with me' ceases to be pious jargon and instead becomes a straightforward description of daily life.

Richard Foster

DECEMBER 28

The Christian way of life does not take away our loneliness; it protects and cherishes it as a precious gift. Sometimes it seems as if we do everything possible to avoid the painful confrontation with our basic human loneliness, and allow ourselves to be trapped by false gods promising immediate satisfaction and quick relief. But perhaps the painful awareness of loneliness is an invitation to transcend our limitations and look beyond the boundaries of our existence. The awareness of loneliness might be a gift we must protect and guard, because our loneliness reveals to us an inner emptiness that can be destructive when misunderstood, but filled with promise for him who can tolerate its sweet pain.

When we are impatient... we ignore what we already know with a deep-seated, intuitive knowledge: that no love or friendship, no intimate embrace or tender kiss, no community, commune or collective, no man or woman, will ever be able to satisfy our desire to be released from our lonely condition.

Henri Nouwen

DECEMBER 29

Let me suggest that the bad things that happen to us in our lives do not have a meaning when they happen to us. They do not happen for any good reason which would cause us to accept them willingly. But we can give them a meaning. We can redeem these tragedies from senselessness by imposing meaning on them. The question we should be asking is not, 'Why did this happen to me? What did I do to deserve this?' That is really an unanswerable pointless question. A better question would be, 'Now that this has happened to me, what am I going to do about it?'...

The facts of life and death are neutral. We, by our responses, give suffering either a positive or a negative meaning. Illness, accidents, human tragedies kill people. But they do not necessarily kill life or faith. If the death and suffering of someone we love makes us bitter, jealous, against all religion, and incapable of happiness, we turn the person who dies into one of the 'devil's martyrs'. If suffering and death in someone close to us brings us to explore the limits of our capacity for strength and love and cheerfulness, if it leads us to discover sources of consolation we never knew before, then we make the person into a witness for the affirmation of life rather than its rejection.

This means… that there is one thing we can still do for those we loved and lost… to let them be witnesses for God and for life, rather than, by our despair and loss of faith, making them 'the devil's martyrs'. The dead depend on us for their redemption and their immortality.

Harold Kushner

DECEMBER 30

Be loyal to the will of the One who draws you by a still small voice. Prepare to listen by clearing your life of noise and clutter. Ask yourself what is your deepest desire.

Do not give ultimate loyalty to anything but the mysterious divine Creator-Lover. So live simply and generously where greed and addiction rule.

Pay close attention simply to what is. Ask the questions that arise from such contemplation, and seek to respond in truth.

Be thankful for small deeds of kindness as well as for greater blessings, and allow the spirit of gratitude to melt the ice of fear and pain. Take time out of time to rest and to be, to celebrate and to laugh.

Be steadfast as you live the commitments you have made. Face illusion and betrayal with truth and courage. Delve ever deeper the mines of trust, forgiveness, and compassion.

Welcome both neighbour and stranger as human beings to be accepted and valued in the same way as you yourself would wish to be received.

Make your contribution to the common good of your own country, and of the one world, of which you are a citizen. Reverence the earth and replenish what you have taken.

Open your heart to kindness and compassion, for yourself and for others. Respond to the lonely with care and tact. Cast out fear by the presence and gentle persistence of prayerful and thoughtful affection. Share the pain of those whose stories reveal harm and shame, and be with them without intrusion or possession.

Refuse to act on feelings of superiority. Shun slogans. Bear the discomfort of what is unresolved. Listen silently to those who are different from yourself, without anxiety or hurry, and so avoid the strident claims of the fanatic and the selfrighteous. Remember that each of us is contained within a whole that is greater than the sum of the parts.

Be expectant of the future, in faith and hope, trusting that it will bring gifts beyond anything you could predict or imagine.

Jim Cotter, 'Ten Invitations'

DECEMBER 31

Planning does not produce vision. Seeking a fresh vision is a spiritual quest that involves living in ambiguity (chaos), waiting on God, dying to old ways, letting the Spirit blow where she will and being resurrected to face a new day in a new way. Grasping a new vision requires 'letting go' and being open to transformation. Planning processes without waiting for the prophetic voice and the new vision, will likely result in restructuring of what is and not transformation.

1995 General Synod Journal of the Anglican Church in Canada

INDEX OF SOURCES

E

Ebner, Christina   Oct 5
Ecclestone, Alan   Aug 24
Edmund of Abingdon   Apr 17
Ehrmann, Max   Jul 20

F

Farrer, Austin   Aug 23
Fleming, Jennifer Baker   Oct 26
Foster, Richard   Dec 27
Fowles, John   Sep 27
Francis of Assisi   Apr 21, Sep 6
Fry, Joan Mary   Oct 11

G

Gateley, Edwina   Dec 24
Giono, Jean   Nov 11
Gore-Booth, Eva   Sep 17
Goudge, Elizabeth   Oct 18, 19
Graveson, Caroline C.   Oct 15
Gregory of Nyssa   Jun 11
Griffin, Emilie   Oct 30
Griffiths, Bede   May 31

H

Hadewijch of Brabant   May 18
Hall, Joseph   Aug 4
Hardy, Thomas   Sep 12
Herbert, George   Jul 5
Hesse, Hermann   Sep 18
Heyward, Carter   Oct 23
Hildegard of Bingen   May 14, 15, Sep 4, 5
Hilton, Walter   May 8, 9

Holland, Henry Scott   Aug 20
Hooker, Richard   Aug 2
Hooley, Teresa   Jul 29
Hopkins, Gerard Manley   Sep 13
Houselander, Caryll   Oct 27

I

Ignatius Loyola   Apr 29, 30
Isaac of Nineveh   Jun 16, 17

J

John of Karpathos   Jun 13
John of the Cross   May 26, 27
Johnson, Josephine   Sep 24
Jones, Alan   Aug 25
Julian of Norwich   May 10, 11

K

Kavanagh, Patrick   Sep 19
Kazantzakis, Nikos   Nov 15
Keenan, Brian   Dec 15
Kempe, Margery   May 12, 13
Kilvert, Francis   Sep 15
Kim Chi Ha   Dec 19
Kushner, Harold   Dec 29

L

Law, William   Aug 11
Lawrence, D.H.   Jul 19
Lessing, Doris   Aug 26
Lewin, Ann   Jul 30
Lewis, C.S.   Aug 22

INDEX OF THEMES

ACKNOWLEDGMENTS

Maria Boulding, *The Coming of God*, SPCK, 1994.

January

1: Revised English Bible © 1989, Oxford and Cambridge University Presses.
2–20, 22–31: The New Revised Standard Version of the Bible, copyright © 1989 by the Division of Christian Education of the National Council of Churches of Christ in the USA.
21: Jim Cotter, *Towards the City: A Version of Psalms 101–150*, Cairns Publications, 1993.

February

1: Authorized version of the Bible (The King James Version), Cambridge University Press (Crown's patentee).
2–17, 20–28: The New Revised Standard Version of the Bible, copyright © 1989 by the Division of Christian Education of the National Council of Churches of Christ in the USA.
18–19: New Jerusalem Bible © 1985 DLT and Doubleday and Co. Inc.

March

1–6: Athanasius, *The Life of Saint Antony*, trans. Robert C. Gregg, Paulist Press, 1980. Used by permission.
7–12: *The Wisdom of the Desert*, trans. Thomas Merton, Sheldon Press, 1974. Copyright © 1960 by The Abbey of Gethsemani, Inc. Reprinted by permission of New Directions Publishing Corp.
13–14: *The Wisdom of the Desert Fathers*, trans. Benedicta Ward, Oxford: SLG Press, 1986.
15–31: *The Sayings of the Desert Fathers*, trans. Benedicta Ward, Mowbray/Cistercian Publications Inc., WMU Station, Kalamazoo, Michigan 49008, USA, 1975.

April

2: *The Confessions of St Patrick*, cited in Joseph Duffy, *Patrick in His Own Words*, Dublin: Veritas, 1972.
3: Adamnan, *The Life of Columba*, cited in *The Divine Office*, vol. III, Collins, Dwyer, Talbot, 1974.
4: K.M. Evans, *A Book of Welsh Saints*, Church in Wales Publications, 1959.
5–7, 9–10: Bede, *A History of the English Church and People*, trans. Leo Sherley-Price, Penguin Classics, 1955, rev. edition 1968. Copyright © 1955, 1968 Leo Sherley-Price. Reproduced by permission of Penguin Books Ltd.
8: Bede, *The Life of Cuthbert*, cited in *The Age of Bede*, trans. J.F. Webb, Penguin, 1988.
11–12: Anselm, *Proslogion*, cited in *The Prayers and Meditations of Saint Anselm*, trans. Benedicta Ward, Penguin Classics, 1973. Copyright © Benedicta Ward. Reproduced by permission of Penguin Books Ltd.
13–14: William of St Thierry, *Three Meditations* cited in *The Cistercian World: Monastic Writings of the Twelfth Century*, trans. Pauline Matarasso, Penguin, 1993.
15–16: Aelred of Rievaulx, *On Spiritual Friendship*, cited in *The Cistercian World*, trans. Pauline Matarasso, Penguin Classics, 1993. Copyright © 1993 Pauline Matarasso. Reproduced by permission of Penguin Books Ltd.
17: Edmund of Abingdon, *The Mirror of St Edmund*, cited in *The English Spirit*, eds Paul Handley, Fiona MacMath, Pat Saunders and Robert van de Weyer, DLT, 1987.
18–19: Bernard of Clairvaux, *Sermon 74 on the Song of Songs*, cited in *The Cistercian World*, trans. Pauline Matarasso, Penguin, 1993.
20: Giovanni di Ceprano, *The Legend of the Three Companions*, cited in *The Little Flowers, Legends, & Lauds*, ed. Otto Karrer, trans. N. Wydenbruck, Sheed & Ward, 1947.
21: 'Reconstruction of the "primitive" rule of Saint Francis', cited in *The Sources for the Life of S. Francis of Assisi*, ed. J.R.H. Moorman, Manchester University Press, 1940.
22: Letter of St Clare to Blessed Agnes of Prague, cited in *Celebrating the Saints*, New York: Pueblo Publishing Co, 1978.
23: Thomas Aquinas, *Summa Theologiae*, cited by Richard Woods, in *Visions of Creation*, ed. Eileen Conn and James Stewart, Godsfield Press, 1995.
24: Angela of Foligno, cited in *The Virago Book of Spirituality*, ed. Sarah Anderson, Virago, 1996.
25–26: Catherine of Siena, *The Dialogue of Catherine of Siena*, trans. Suzanne Noffke, Paulist Press, 1980. Used by permission of Paulist Press.

27–28: Thomas à Kempis, *The Imitation of Christ*, trans. Leo Sherley-Price, Penguin, 1952.

29–30: Ignatius of Loyola, *The Autobiography*, cited in *Ignatius of Loyola: The Spiritual Exercises and Selected Works*, ed. George Ganss, trans. Parmananda R. Divarkar, Paulist Press, 1991.

May

1: Evelyn Underhill, *The Spiritual Life*, Hodder and Stoughton, 1937.

2–3: Evelyn Underhill, *Practical Mysticism*, J.M. Dent, 1914.

4–5: Richard Rolle, *The Fire of Love*, trans. Clifton Wolters, Penguin, 1972.

6–7: *The Cloud of Unknowing*, ed. James Walsh, Paulist Press, 1981. Used by permission.

8–9: Walter Hilton, *The Ladder of Perfection*, trans. Leo Sherley-Price, Penguin, 1957.

10–11: Julian of Norwich, *Revelations of Divine Love*, in *Julian of Norwich: Showings*, trans. Edmund Colledge and James Walsh, SPCK, 1978. Published by Paulist Press.

12–13: Margery Kempe, *The Book of Margery Kempe*, trans. B.A. Windeatt, Penguin, 1985.

14–15: *Hildegard of Bingen: An Anthology*, ed. and introduced by Fiona Bowie and Oliver Davies, trans. Robert Carver, SPCK, 1990.

16–18: *Beguine Spirituality, An Anthology*, ed. and introduced by Fiona Bowie, trans. Oliver Davies, SPCK, 1989. Published in the US, Canada and the Philippines by Crossroad Publishing.

19–21: *Meditations with Meister Eckhart*, introduction and versions by Matthew Fox, Bear and Co., 1983. Copyright © 1983 Bear and Co., Santa Fe, NM. Reprinted with permission.

22: *The Rhineland Mystics*, trans. Oliver Davies, SPCK, 1989.

23–25: Teresa of Avila, *The Interior Castle*, trans. Kieran Kavanaugh and Otilio Rodriguez, Paulist Press, 1979. Used by permission.

26–27: *You Set My Spirit Free. A 40-day Journey in the Company of John of the Cross*, paraphrased by David Hazard, Minneapolis: Bethany House Publishers, 1994.

28: *The New Golden Treasury of English Verse*, ed. Edward Leeson, Macmillan, 1994.

29: Lucie-Christine, *Spiritual Journal of Lucie-Christine*, London, 1915.

30: Charles de Foucauld, *Meditations of a Hermit*, Burns and Oates, 1930.

31: *The Golden String*, by Bede Griffiths, HarperCollins, 1954.

June

1–4: Catherine de Hueck Doherty, *Poustinia*, Madonna House Publications, 1993.

5–9: *The Way of a Pilgrim*, trans. R.M. French, SPCK, 1930.

10: Basil of Caesarea, *Treatise on the Holy Spirit*, cited in Olivier Clément, *The Roots of Christian Mysticism*, New City, 1993.

11: Gregory of Nyssa, *Second Homily on the Song of Songs*, trans. Theodore Berkeley and Jeremy Hummerstone.

12: Dionysius the Pseudo-Areopagite, cited in Olivier Clément, *The Roots of Christian Mysticism*, New City, 1993.

13: John of Karpathos, 'Texts for the Monks in India', in *The Philokalia*, vol. 1, trans. G.E.H. Palmer, Philip Sherrard and Kallistos Ware, Faber and Faber, 1979.

14: Maximus the Confessor, cited in Olivier Clément, *The Roots of Christian Mysticism*, New City, 1993.

15: Dorotheus of Gaza, cited in *Seasons of the Spirit*, ed. George Every, Richard Harries and Kallistos Ware, SPCK, 1984.

16–17: Isaac of Nineveh, cited in Olivier Clément, *The Roots of Christian Mysticism*, New City, 1993.

18: Dimitrii of Rostov, cited in *The Art of Prayer: An Orthodox Anthology*, ed. Igumen Chariton of Valamo, trans. E. Kadloubovsky and E.M. Palmer, Faber and Faber Ltd, 1966.

19–22: *Writings from the Philokalia on Prayer of the Heart*, trans. E. Kadloubovsky and G.E.H. Palmer, Faber and Faber Ltd, 1951.

23–24: Theophan the Recluse, cited in *The Art of Prayer: An Orthodox Anthology*, ed. Igumen Chariton of Valamo, trans. E. Kadloubovsky and E.M. Palmer, Faber and Faber Ltd, 1966.

25–27: Fyodor Dostoevsky, *The Brothers Karamazov*, 1880.

28: Anthony Bloom, cited in *Sobornost incorporating Eastern Churches Review 1.2*, Fellowship of St Alban and St Sergius, 1979.

29: Anthony Bloom, *Living Prayer*, DLT, 1966.

30: Anthony Bloom, *School for Prayer*, DLT, 1970.

July

1: Pablo Neruda, *Isla Negra: A Notebook*, trans. Alastair Reid, New York: The Noonday Press, 1981. Translation copyright © 1970, 1979, 1981 by Alistair Reid. Used by permission of the publisher.

2: Dante Alighieri, cited in James Collins, *Meditations with Dante Alighieri*, Bear & Company, 1984.

16: *The Poems of Emily Dickinson*, ed. T.H. Johnson, The Bellknap Press, Harvard.

17: Francis Thompson, cited in *The Oxford Book of Mystical Verse*, OUP, 1917.

18: Amy Carmichael, *Toward Jerusalem*. Copyright © The Dohnavur Fellowship, UK, published by the Christian Literature Crusade, USA.

19: D.H. Lawrence, *The Complete Poems of D.H. Lawrence*, ed. V. de Sola Pinto and F.W. Roberts. Copyright © 1964, 1971 by Angelo Ravagli and C.M. Weekley, Executors of the Estate of Mrs Frieda Lawrence Ravagli. Used by permission of Viking Penguin, a division of Penguin Putnam Inc. and Lawrence Pollinger Ltd.

20: Max Ehrmann, *The Desiderata of Happiness*, Souvenir Press, 1986. Copyright © 1948 Bertha K. Ehrmann. All rights reserved. Reprinted by permission of Robert L. Bell, Melrose, MA 02176, USA.

21: R.S. Thomas, *Mass for Hard Times*, Bloodaxe Books, 1992.

22: Dylan Thomas, *The Poems of Dylan Thomas*, J.M. Dent. Copyright © 1952 by Dylan Thomas. Reproduced by permission of David Higham Associates Ltd. Published in the US and Canada by New Directions Publishing Corp.

23: William Stafford, *Holding Onto The Grass*, Weatherlight Press, 1994. Copyright © The Estate of William Stafford.

24: Kathleen Raine, *Collected Poems*, Allen and Unwin, 1981. Reproduced by permission HarperCollinsPublishers Ltd.

25: Sydney Carter, *The Two-Way Clock*, Galliard, 1969. Copyright © Stainer & Bell Ltd.

26–27: Edwin Muir and Chad Walsh cited in *Modern Religious Verse*, ed. Timothy Beaumont, Studio Vista, 1966.

29: Teresa Hooley, cited in *Let There Be God*, ed. T.H. Parker and F.J. Teskey, Religious Education Press, 1968.

30: Ann Lewin, *Candles and Kingfishers*, The Methodist Publishing House.

31: Tony Lucas, cited in *The Least Things*, Exeter: Stride Publications, 1989.

August

1: *Life of Thomas More*, cited in *The Fourth Lesson*, ed. Christopher Campling, DLT, 1973.

2: Richard Hooker, *The Laws of Ecclesiastical Polity*, 1593.

3: Lancelot Andrewes, *Sermon Four on Repentance: Ash Wednesday 1619*, cited in *The English Spirit*, eds Paul Handley, Fiona MacMath, Pat Saunders and Robert van de Weyer, DLT, 1987.

4–5, 6, 9: Joseph Hall, Sir Thomas Browne, Jeremy Taylor and William Beveridge cited in *Anglicanism*, ed. More and Cross, SPCK, 1935.

7: Richard Baxter, cited in *The English Spirit*, eds Paul Handley, Fiona MacMath, Pat Saunders and Robert van de Weyer, DLT, 1987.

8: John Bunyan, *The Pilgrim's Progress*.

10: Thomas Traherne, cited in *Poems, Centuries and Three Thanksgivings*, ed. Ridler, OUP, 1966.

11: William Law, *A Serious Call to a Devout and Holy Life*, 1728.

12: John Wesley, cited in David Butler, *Methodists and Papists*, DLT, 1995.

13: John Woolman, cited in *Quaker Spirituality*, ed. Douglas Steere, Paulist Press, 1984.

14: Charles Simeon, cited in *All in the End is Harvest*, ed. Agnes Whitaker, DLT, 1984.

15: James Henry Newman, *Hymns Ancient and Modern*.

16: James Martineau, *Hours of Thought on Sacred Things*, vol. 1, Longmans, Green, Reader and Dyer, 1880.

17: Elizabeth Barrett Browning, *Aurora Leigh*, 1857.

18: Charles Spurgeon, 'The Holy Spirit in Our Ministry', *Lectures to My Students*, American Tract Society, n.d.

19: Charles Spurgeon, 'The Chaff Driven Away', *Sermons of C.H. Spurgeon of London*, Funk and Wagnalls, n.d.

20: Henry Scott Holland, 'The King of Terrors', *Facts of the Faith*, Longmans and Co, 1919.

21: John Chapman, 'Spiritual Letters', cited in *The English Spirit*, eds Paul Handley, Fiona MacMath, Pat Saunders and Robert van de Weyer, DLT, 1987.

22: C.S. Lewis, *Mere Christianity*, Geoffrey Bles, 1952.

23: Austin Farrer, *Saving Belief*, Hodder and Stoughton, 1964.

24: Alan Ecclestone, *Spirituality for Today*, ed. Eric James, SCM, 1968.

25: Alan Jones, *Soul Making*, SCM Press, 1985.

26: Doris Lessing, *The Four Gated City*, Grafton Books, 1972.

27: John Robinson, 'Learning from Cancer', in Eric James, *The Life of Bishop John A.T. Robinson*, Collins, 1987.

28: John Robinson, cited in Shelagh Brown, *Drawing Near to the City*, Triangle, 1984.

29: John V. Taylor, *The Go-Between God: The Holy Spirit and Christian Mission*, SCM, 1972.

30: J. Neville Ward, *The Use of Praying*, Methodist Publishing House, 1968.

31: H.A. Williams, *The True Wilderness*, Constable, 1965.

September

1–3: Revised English Bible © 1989, Oxford and Cambridge University Presses.

4–5: Hildegard of Bingen, cited in Gabriele Uhlein, *Meditations with Hildegard of Bingen*, Bear & Co., 1983. Copyright © 1983 Bear & Co., Sante Fe, NM. Reprinted with permission.

6: Francis of Assisi, cited in *Celebrating Common Prayer*, Mowbray, 1992.

7: *Jacopone da Todi*, trans. Serge and Elizabeth Hughes, Paulist Press, 1982. Used by permission.

8: Dafydd ap Gwilym, cited in *Oxford Book of Welsh Verse*, OUP, 1977. Published by Faber and Faber Ltd.

11: Henry D. Thoreau, *Walden*, W.W. Norton & Co., 1992.

12: Thomas Hardy, 'The Darkling Thrush', Macmillan.

15: *Kilvert's Diary*, ed. William Plomer, Jonathan Cape, 1960.

16: Evelyn Underhill, *Theophanies*, J.M. Dent, 1916.

18: Hermann Hesse, cited in *News of the Universe: Poems of Twofold Consciousness*, trans. Robert Bly, Sierra Club Books, San Francisco, 1980. Copyright © 1980, 1995.

19: Patrick Kavanagh, cited in *Irish Poetry of Faith and Doubt*, ed. John F. Deane, Wolfhound Press, 1991. Reprinted by kind permission of the Trustees of the Estate of Patrick Kavanagh, c/o Peter Fallon, Literary Agent, Loughcrew, Oldcastle, Co, Meath, Ireland.

20: Thomas Merton, *Raids on the Unspeakable*, New Directions Publishing, 1966. Copyright © 1966 by the Abbey of Gethsemani, Inc. Reprinted by permission of New Directions Publishing Corp.

21: Helder Câmara, *A Thousand Reasons for Living*, ed. Jose de Broucker, trans. Alan Neame, DLT, 1981. Published and copyright © 1981 Darton Longman and Todd Ltd and used by permission of the publishers. Published in the US and Canada by Fortress Press and Augsburg.

22: Thomas Berry, cited in *To Honour the Earth*, by Dorothy Maclean, HarperSanFrancisco, 1991.

23: Annie Dillard, *Pilgrim at Tinker Creek*, Picador, 1976.

24: Josephine Johnson, cited in *Love is my Meaning*, ed. Elizabeth Basset, DLT, 1973. Published and copyright © 1973, 1986 Darton Longman and Todd Ltd and used by permission of the publishers.

25: Wendell Berry, *The Collected Poems 1957–1982*, Harcourt Brace and Co.

26: Wendell Berry, *The Collected Poems 1957–1982*, North Point Press, 1984.

27: John Fowles and Frank Horvat (photographer), *The Tree*, Aurum Press, 1979.

28: Anonymous, cited in *Earth Prayers*, ed. Elizabeth Roberts and Elias Amidon, HarperCollins US, 1991.

29: William Stafford, *An Oregon Message*, Harper & Row, 1987.

30: Sally McFague, *Models of God: Theology for an Ecological, Nuclear Age*, Fortress Press, 1987.

October

1: Anna Julia Cooper, *A Voice from the South by a Black Woman from the South*, Xenia, Ohio: Aldine Printing House, 1892.

2–4: Revised English Bible © 1989, Oxford and Cambridge University Presses.

5, 8, 12: Christina Ebner, Marguerite d'Angouleme and Emily Dickinson, cited in Gerda Lerner, *The Creation of Feminist Consciousness*, OUP, 1993.

6: Marguerite d'Oingt, cited in *Medieval Women's Visionary Literature*, ed. Elizabeth Alvida Petroff, OUP, 1986.

7: Christine de Pizan, cited in *The Book of the City of Ladies*, trans. Earl Jeffrey Richards, New York: Persea Books, 1982.

9–10, 17: Josephine Butler, Hannah Whitall Smith, Dorothy Day, cited in *Women's Wisdom through the Ages*, ed. Mary Horner and Vinita Hampton Wright, Hodder and Stoughton, 1994.

11: Joan Mary Fry, *The Communion of Life*, Swarthmore Lecture, Headley Brothers, 1910.

13–14: Thérèse of Lisieux, cited in T.N. Taylor, *Saint Thérèse of Lisieux, The Little Flower of Jesus*, Burns and Oates, 1944.

15: Caroline Graveson, 'Religion and Culture' (Swarthmore Lecture, 1937), cited in *Christian Faith and Practice in the Experience of the Society of Friends*, London Yearly Meeting of the Religious Society of Friends, 1960, no. 463.

16: Lilian Smith, cited in *The Virago Book of Spirituality*, ed. Sarah Anderson, Virago, 1996.

18–19: Elizabeth Goudge, cited in *A Vision of God*, ed. Christine Rawlins, Spire, 1990.

20: Dorothy L. Sayers, 'The Human-Not-Quite-Human', in *Unpopular Opinions*, Gollancz, 1946.

21: Ruth Burgess, 'The Desert', in *Celebrating Women*, ed. Hannah Ward, Jennifer Wild and Janet Morley, SPCK, 1995. Editorial matter copyright © 1995 Hannah Ward, Jennifer Wild and Janet Morley. Reproduced by permission of Morehouse Publishing, Harrisburg, PA.

22: Janet Morley, *All Desires Known*, SPCK, 1992. Copyright © 1988, 1992 Janet Morley. Reproduced by permission of Morehouse Publishing, Harrisburg, PA.

23: Carter Heyward, *The Redemption of God: A Theology of Mutual Relation*, Washington DC: University Press of America, 1982.

24–25: Anonymous, cited in Kathleen Fischer, *Women at the Well*, SPCK, 1989.

26: Jennifer Baker Fleming, *Stopping Wife Abuse*, Anchor Press, New York, 1979. Copyright © 1979 Jennifer Baker Fleming. Used by permission of Doubleday, a division of Bantam Doubleday Dell Publishing Group, Inc.

27: Caryll Houselander, *The Reed of God*, Sheed and Ward, 1955.

28: Anne Morrow Lindbergh, *Gift from the Sea*, Chatto and Windus, 1955.

29: Simone Weil, *Waiting on God*, Routledge and Kegan Paul, 1951.

30: Emilie Griffin, cited in *Women's Wisdom through the Ages*, Hodder and Stoughton, 1994.

31: Rosemary Radford Ruether, *To Change the World*, New York: Crossroad, 1981.

November

1–3: Revised English Bible © 1989, Oxford and Cambridge University Presses.

4: Margaret Fishback Powers, *Footprints*, HarperCollins.

11: Author's retelling of a story from Jean Giono, *The Man who Planted Hope and Grew Happiness*, Friends of Nature, 1967.

12–13: William J. Bausch, *Storytelling: Imagination and Faith*, Twenty Third Publications, 1984.

14: Mark Pryce, cited in James Woodward, *Embracing the Chaos: Theological Responses to AIDS*, SPCK, 1990.

15: Nikos Kazantzakis, *Zorba the Greek*, Faber & Faber, 1961.

20–27: Anthony de Mello, *The Prayer of the Frog* vol. 1, Anand India: Gujarat Sahitya Prakash, 1987.

28–29: Anthony de Mello, cited in Carlos Valles, *Mastering Sadhana: On Retreat with Anthony de Mello*, Fount, 1988.

December

1: Mary Mother Clare, *Learning to Pray*, Marshall Pickering, 1970.

2: W.H. Vanstone, *Love's Endeavour, Love's Expense*, DLT, 1977.

3: Cecil Collins, *Meditations, Poems, Pages from a Sketchbook*, Golgonooza Press, 1997.

4: Jean Vanier, *The Broken Body: Journey to Wholeness*, DLT, 1988. Copyright © 1988 Jean Vanier. Published and copyright © 1988 Darton Longman and Todd Ltd and used by permission of the publishers. Published in Canada by the Anglican Book Centre, 600 Jarris Street, Toronto, Ontario, Canada M4Y 2J6. Used with permission. Published in Australia and New Zealand by St Paul's Publications (Australia).

5: Anonymous, printed in *Catholic AIDS Link Newsletter*, October 1990.

6: Paulo Coelho, *The Pilgrimage*, Thorsons, 1997.

7: John Payne Cook, copyright © 1998.

8: Pierre Teilhard de Chardin, cited in Margaret Guenther, *Holy Listening*, DLT, 1992. Published by Editions du Seuil and HarperCollins US.

9: Marianne Williamson, *A Return to Love: Reflections on the Principles of a Course in Miracles*, Harper Mass Market, 1994. As quoted by Nelson Mandela, in his 1994 Inaugural Speech.

10: Mary Oliver, *Dream Work*, New York: The Atlantic Monthly Press, 1986.

11: Kathleen Raine, cited in *Bloodaxe Book of Contemporary Women Poets*, ed. Jeni Couzyn, Bloodaxe Books, 1985.

12–13: Rainer Maria Rilke, *Letters to a Young Poet*, trans. Joan M. Burnham, New World Library, 1992.

14: Maria Boulding, *The Coming of God*, SPCK, 1994.

15: Brian Keenan, *An Evil Cradling*, Hutchinson, 1992.

16–17: Esse Chardin and Maya Angelou, cited in *The Feminine Face of God*, ed. Sherry Ruth Anderson and Patricia Hopkins, Bantam Books, 1992.

18: Jim Cotter, *Pleasure, Pain and Passion*, Cairns Publications, 1988.

19, 21: Kim Chi Ha and Anthony de Mello, cited in *The Bible through Asian Eyes*, ed. Masao Takenaka and Ron O'Grady, Pace Publishing, 1991.

20: James K. Baxter, 'Lord, Holy Spirit', OUP.

22: Thomas Merton, *Seeds of Contemplation*, A. Clarke Books, 1972.

23: Thomas Merton, *New Seeds of Contemplation*, New York: New Directions, 1962. Copyright © 1961 The Abbey of Gethsemani, Inc. Reprinted by permission of New Directions Publishing Corp.

24: Edwina Gateley, cited in *There Was No Path So I Trod One*, California: Source Books, 1996. Reproduced by permission.

25–26: John Main, *Moment of Christ*, DLT, 1984.

27: Richard Foster, *Meditative Prayer*, Inter-Varsity Christian Fellowship, 1984.

28: Henri Nouwen, *The Wounded Healer*, Image Books, 1979.

29: Harold Kushner, *When Bad Things Happen to Good People*, Pan, 1982.

30: Jim Cotter and the Cairns Network, *By Heart for the Millennium*.

31: 1995 General Synod Journal of the Anglican Church in Canada.